# He Made the Stars Also

# He Made the Stars Also

*Seven Stories that Had to Be Told*

Cole Huffman

WIPF & STOCK · Eugene, Oregon

HE MADE THE STARS ALSO
Seven Stories that Had to Be Told



Wipf & Stock
An Imprint of Wipf and Stock Publishers
199 W. 8th Ave., Suite 3
Eugene, OR 97401

www.wipfandstock.com

PAPERBACK ISBN: 978-1-4982-8656-5
HARDCOVER ISBN: 978-1-62032-752-4
EBOOK ISBN: 978-1-62032-021-1

Manufactured in the U.S.A. MAY 15, 2019

For Dad,
He who began a good work in us brings it to completion.

He determines the number of the stars;
he gives to all of them their names.

—PSALM 147:4

# Contents

# Acknowledgements

IT'S BEEN SAID THAT books are never really done. They are simply due. Perhaps the same could be said of preaching. As a preacher, I live under a creative deadline. Sunday is always coming. The sermon is delivered but shelved afterwards. In the week that follows, I have to move on to the next one. No sermon ever feels quite done.

This book began as sermons preached in my church, First Evan in Memphis. In book form now, these messages get to live on long past the summer Sundays I preached them. Many have encouraged me through the process of converting sermons to chapters. I want to especially thank my fellow elders on our session for granting me a month of study leave to get it started.

My wife Lynn is a delight to share life with and I am grateful for all her support. This book is dedicated to my dad. Dad's cancer progressed as work on this neared completion. I needed the companionship I got with the death-defeating Jesus.

My twelfth grade English teacher, Mrs. Palmer, never knew the seeds she planted when she once wrote on an essay I turned in, "You should write, Cole." I knew whenever I did I wanted to acknowledge her for that, and this seems a good place.

Thank you to the editors at Wipf and Stock for giving me the opportunity to publish with them. My mom being a career editor, I know what good editors do for authors, particularly first-timers.

Thanks be to God for the great things he has done.

# Introduction

Allow me to introduce two images to you. One is from art, the other from athletics.

From art: Imagine a small brown leather suitcase lying on its side on a white table in an art gallery. The artist cut a hole in it and affixed a label: *Look inside*. You do and see infinite space full of stars, the optical effect of two acid-spotted mirrors stuck to the top and bottom of the case, lit up by tiny bulbs.[1]

From athletics: Think of a batting rotation in baseball. The first player up to bat is called the leadoff. He's usually one of the team's best hitters and a fast runner. The cleanup batter is the power hitter. Should the first three batters make base, perhaps the cleanup batter can grand slam them all home.

John gave us a suitcase of stars and a batting rotation in his recollection of seven signs. Miracles Jesus did. Not ordinary everyday occurrences, though they happened in everyday settings, but extraordinary events nonetheless. Wonderments. Creative supernatural acts meant to uniquely authenticate Jesus' credibility as God in flesh.

The miracles of Jesus were marvels in the moment, but they also pay it forward. His miraculous power creates anticipation of his kingdom coming in fullness. Israel was suffering doubly in Jesus' day. Not just from the universal weight of sin, but Israel had a specific covenant arrangement with God, the terms of which threatened curses for disobedience.[2]

1. Macdonald, *H is for Hawk*, 58.

2. Deut 28:15–28.

The prevalence of disease and demonization in first-century Israel, as well as having to live under the foreign domination of Rome, evidenced God's judgment in consequence. It felt like the stars were flaming out over Israel. Each miracle of Jesus was a rallying of hopes that God was still bigger than Caesar, and a glimpse at a future renewal to come when the messiah of God reigned.

Each miracle of Jesus says *look inside*. Jesus turned water into wine. Among the seven John features, that one is in the leadoff spot. The other six signs accompanying it are each and all designed to get us "on base" with God through Christ. The pinnacle sign is the one that gets us home: the bodily resurrection of Jesus from his death on a cross.

Although not numbered among the traditional seven signs in John's Gospel—they end at Lazarus' resurrection in John 11—the resurrection of Jesus is *the sign* by which we believe in him and have life in his name. I'm not a Christian because I believe Jesus turned water into wine or walked on water (although it would be hard to be a Christian and not believe it). I'm a Christian because I believe Jesus walked out of his tomb. Paul says if that didn't happen our faith is futile.[3]

This book is an invitation to look inside John's selected miracle stories. Why only seven? John says Jesus "did many signs in the presence of the disciples, which are not written in this book" (John 20:30). There are, by scholarly count, thirty-eight miracles recorded in the Gospels.[4] Picking out seven to narrate could be John's hat tip to the seven-day creation account of Genesis, Jesus' prior creative working.[5] But even if John recalled seventy-seven sign stories in his Gospel, the seven he chose are for giving us a look inside new creation at work: "these are written so that you may believe that Jesus is the Christ, the Son of God, and that by believing you may have life in his name" (John 20:31).

3. 1 Cor 15:14.

4. Dickson, *Spectator's Guide to Jesus*, 42.

5. Col 1:15–20.

## Insiders with God

A believer in Jesus becomes an insider with God, seeking his way and will. Life in Jesus' name is living in anticipation of God's future, longing for his appearing when he makes all things new.[6] It is faith in him developing into love for him. Desiring God for God, not just for what he gives.

Belief in miracles, even witnessing them, does not automatically produce belief in Jesus as the Son of God. Some connect causality to miracles: that a miraculous action *must yield* a believing result. But Jesus' enemies, while not denying his supernatural power, didn't believe in him. Many, even among the wonderstruck, eventually turned on him.

Jesus himself downplayed his wonderworking because a miracle itself is not the point. Miracles serve belief in Christ like an index finger serves to trace out constellations in the night sky. One looks to where the finger is pointing, not the finger.[7] Miracles appreciated for aesthetic merits only miss the point.

The *miracle-worker* is the point. Who is he? From where does he get his power? What does he want from us in response?

> Jesus calls miracles *signs*. The writer of Hebrews calls them *shadows*. Miracles are meant to point to something bigger, more real, more alive, than themselves. But when faith comes to depend on a miracle, it ends up mistaking the sign for the destination, the shadow for the substance, the nourishment for the soil itself. Miracles, for all their power to shore up faith, are themselves rickety things, flimsy, porous. They can only point, mutely, to the place we need to go. They can only cast, coolly, the flat dark shape, devoid of detail, of the thing we need to embrace. At best, they are silhouettes, showing us in outline, without color or feature, the reality we need to behold. They are fingerprints of God, a clue to His presence, but they are not His hand.[8]

6. 2 Cor 5:17; Rev 21:5.
7. Lamott, *Hallelujah Anyway*, 142.
8. Buchanan, *Things Unseen*, 132.

Every sign John presents in his sequence points to Jesus himself. He is the one sent from God to reconcile human beings to God and open to us the his-name-on-us kind of life. In each chapter that follows, I want to tell Jesus' story using the seven miracle events John chose to narrate Jesus' life, work, and identity.

## The Super-Natural

Here and now, where we live and work and play, what difference does life in Jesus' name make? Life is full of mundane tasks and disappointments. What difference does Jesus' wonderworking make to the grief we bear? What does life in his name mean to those who bear the burden of hoping, waiting for longings to be fulfilled?

As Frederick Buechner put it, it is not objective proof of God's existence that most of us believers want, but a real experience of God's presence:

> What we need to know, of course, is not just that God exists, not just that beyond the steely brightness of the stars there is a cosmic intelligence of some kind that keeps the whole show going, but that there is a God right here in the thick of our day-to-day lives who may not be writing messages about himself in the stars but in one way or another is trying to get messages through our blindness as we move around down here knee-deep in the fragrant muck and misery and marvel of the world. It is no objective proof of God's existence that we want but the experience of God's presence. This is the miracle we are really after, and that is also, I think, the miracle we really get.[9]

Life for now is a tough hill to climb. We wonder at times if we'll make it. The game can seem rigged against us.

*The Natural*, starring Robert Redford, told the story of a gifted baseball player in the 1930s. Roy Hobbs could send baseballs into virtual orbit. His major league debut at bat, he hit the pitch so hard the cover came off the ball. As the story goes, Hobbs would

9. Quoted in Manning, *Ragamuffin Gospel*, 93.

have been the greatest hitter of all time if not for being the victim of attempted murder early in his career. He survived a gunshot, but the bullet lodged in his stomach, deteriorating the lining over time. Regrets did the same in his heart.

Before a key playoff series, complications from food poisoning put Hobbs' in the hospital. Doctors told him his playing days were over. Undeterred, he rose from his sick bed in time to play in the pivotal game. But he was bleeding internally.

In addition to his physical agony, the corrupt team owner was blackmailing Hobbs into throwing the game. Hobbs also knew he had a son in the stands he'd never met. As his last at-bat arrived, the world was on Roy Hobbs' shoulders. He was his team's only chance to win the pennant. Staring him down from the mound was a fireball ace.

Strike one was smoke.

Hobbs connected with strike two, sending the ball deep but foul. The impact split his legendary bat, "Wonderboy," in two. The batboy brought him another, a bat Hobbs helped him make.

The catcher noticed Hobbs bleeding through his jersey at the beltline. He signaled to the pitcher: curve it low, fast, and inside.

Hobbs rocketed that pitch off the substitute bat. The ball carried high above the outfield upper deck and smashed into one of the lights, starting a chain reaction of gas stadium lights exploding. As he crossed home plate for the last time, the stadium was going dark except for star-like sparks showering Hobbs and his celebrating teammates.

A sportscaster would call that a miraculous finish. It's not in truth. And yet every hero story like *The Natural* is an echo, a familiar tune, of something that thrills us deep inside. When we see someone heroically great at what they do, we can't help but think of one greater.

Jesus was the natural at the supernatural. He was the God-man for whom nothing was too difficult. We know Jesus did the impossible, again and again. G. K. Chesterton once observed that God never tires of saying, "Do it again!" to the sun and moon every morning and evening, because God is strong enough to exult in monotony.[10]

Baseball can seem monotonous until you witness a walk-off home run in the ninth inning. The stadium shakes under your feet. Something powerful is happening. I suppose miracles can be monotonous too in that we are familiar with the ones John picked to record. They will not be new to many readers. But they are part of the reason why we expect the renewal of all things when Jesus returns.

> Throughout history, Christian faith has always involved a restless hope—a hope captured perfectly in the prayer "Your kingdom come." The previews of that kingdom which the miracles of Jesus provide have usually made Christ's followers dissatisfied with the way things are and desperate for the way things Christ said they would be. Christian hope is thus *confidently restless*: it praises God for the preview (in Jesus' life) and pleads for the finale (in the "kingdom come"), when evil will be overthrown, humanity healed and creation itself renewed.[11]

That is what I hope you'll find in the seven sign stories John gave us: Jesus' power and glory. Jesus' grace and truth. Life in his name held out to us and gained for us.

Look inside.

10. Chesterton, *Orthodoxy*, 60.

11. Dickson, *Spectator's Guide to Jesus*, 50.

# John 2:1–11

On the third day there was a wedding at Cana in Galilee, and the mother of Jesus was there. 2 Jesus also was invited to the wedding with his disciples. 3 When the wine ran out, the mother of Jesus said to him, “They have no wine.” 4 And Jesus said to her, “Woman, what does this have to do with me? My hour has not yet come.” 5 His mother said to the servants, “Do whatever he tells you.”

6 Now there were six stone water jars there for the Jewish rites of purification, each holding twenty or thirty gallons.[a] 7 Jesus said to the servants, “Fill the jars with water.” And they filled them up to the brim. 8 And he said to them, “Now draw some out and take it to the master of the feast.” So they took it. 9 When the master of the feast tasted the water now become wine, and did not know where it came from (though the servants who had drawn the water knew), the master of the feast called the bridegroom 10 and said to him, “Everyone serves the good wine first, and when people have drunk freely, then the poor wine. But you have kept the good wine until now.” 11 This, the first of his signs, Jesus did at Cana in Galilee, and manifested his glory. And his disciples believed in him.

# 1

# The Wine of Astonishment

Think of it! The Word was made Flesh and not one of the journalists of those days even knew it was happening!

—Georges Bernanos[1]

I was told if I preached to broken hearts I'd never lack an audience. Life experience is not unanimous, of course. It's not pain and sorrow out there all the time. There are happy birthdays and above average children and short lines at the DMV. There are police officers who let you off with a warning and extra savings on already low sale prices.

Brokenheartedness is a stubborn fact of life, however. If you haven't been brokenhearted yet, you will be. We all get to experience the bitter taste of disappointment.

John's astonishment over the many things Jesus did—"the world itself could not contain the books that would be written" (John 21:25)—applies also to our collective disappointments with life and living. It's dizzying how often things can go wrong in this world. This is the through line in the story of human life east of Eden.

1. Bernanos, *Diary*, 210.

"O God, you have rejected us, broken our defenses; you have been angry; oh, restore us." You don't hear many sermons begin like Psalm 60 does. *God has broken our hearts!* But many a sermon-goer *feels* Psalm 60. "You have made your people see hard things; you have given us wine to drink that made us stagger" (or "wine of astonishment," as the old KJV puts it).

A wedding party is supposed to be a place free of trouble. Too much planning goes into it to risk anything haphazard. Everything is supposed to be just right. But not even the partygoer is immune from the reach of disappointment in a fallen world. Inexplicably, the wine ran out that festive night in Cana. Jesus' first recorded miracle was saving a party from ruin.

Years ago, fresh out of college, I collapsed at a friend's wedding. I perform weddings now, but back then I was a groomsman. We were deep into summer in Mississippi. Someone forgot to turn on the church's air conditioner until an hour before the service. I hadn't learned yet to not lock my knees when standing up for a long time. I was a little hungry too, so I didn't stand a chance in the bouquet-withering humidity (the reason we Southerners have our charming accents, by the way).

The college fullback behind me caught my fall. "Don't move, man!" he said when I came to on the floor. Looks of disappointment were on the faces of the Phi Mu sisters of Mississippi State University, occupying the first three rows of pews to my left. Their sister's wedding wasn't going to be perfect after all, thanks to me, the fainter.

Sometimes I use John 2:1–11 as a wedding text. I tell the couple before me not to expect sunshine always. The marriage covenant they're entering is binding for a reason. There are times one will want out. Even when a couple beautifies their union well, the wine will, metaphorically, run out on them. They will have their share of disappointments in life, perhaps even brokenheartedness.

At some point, at some time, at some place life will not work for us. We can plot this along a sorrow-to-sighing continuum. Sometimes when the wine runs out it's truly anguishing (sorrow). Other times it's more an aggravation (sighing).

In *So You've Been Publicly Shamed*, British journalist Jon Ronson profiles people shredded by public opinion buzzsaws for everything from plagiarism to ill-advised attempts at humor on social media. In the fiascoes Ronson narrates, people found themselves under an avalanche of scrutiny and outcry against themselves, usually disproportionate to their actual offense. Some lost jobs, friends. In each case they felt their lives ripped apart at the seams by people they didn't even know.

The European Court of Justice delivered a judgment called the "Right to be Forgotten" ruling. It was vague in detail, but made provision for people in Europe to formally petition Google to de-index any online information a person deemed "inadequate, irrelevant, or no longer relevant" in regard to themselves. Critics cried censorship, but within three months of the court ruling, seventy thousand people had applied to be forgotten.[2]

Seventy thousand takers might make us deeply sorrowful. It might make us only sigh. But it says a lot of us feel almost married to our mistakes. And if troubles mount, a general sense of foreboding can set in like fog on us. No matter what we do to prevent it, life will still go wrong at points for us. The wine will run out.

## The Good, the Very Good, and the Glory

Weddings in a town like Cana were more of a community event, open to everyone. The pressure on weddings now is for the reception to be creative. High wow factor: like a dessert wall custom-built with pegs wreathed by designer donuts, or placeholders made from a tree the groom cut down himself, the couple's heart-shaped monogram carved into each one. The pressure on weddings in Jesus' time was on the host—to have everything right so he didn't have to resort to creativity.

Each miracle Jesus did is a creative act. As I'm partial to concise definitions, I like the one C. S. Lewis gave when he defined a miracle to be "interference with nature by a supernatural power."[3]

2. Ronson, *So You've Been*, 203.

3. Lewis, *Miracles*, 5.

If one thinks nature is all there is, he denies the possibility of miracles (supernaturalism) outright. But if one believes there is a God responsible for the laws nature obeys, then miracles are possible, even if we never observe one.

Lewis's word choice, "interference," can make us think of things clunky or awkward or intrusive. The supernaturalism of Jesus was agile, and in this miracle in John 2, lavishly generous. He creatively interfered with the metabolism of water to render it a unique Galilean vintage. Instantly. No pressing. No aging.

Wine is not a complicated thing. It's fermented grape juice. But the properties of wine are complex. Even the properties of plain old water are mindboggling on their own: "In eighteen milliliters of water (about two swallows full), there are $6x10^{23}$ molecules of H2O. How much is $6x10^{23}$? A good computer can carry out ten million counts per second. It would take that computer two billion years to count to $6x10^{23}$."[4]

"The conscious water saw its Master and blushed," is how the poet Alexander Pope described the scene in John 2. Whether our minds are blown by the metabolic science or drawn to the poetic, the result was generous. Jesus produced the equivalent of about 750 bottles of fine Cabernet Sauvignon.

There are two stories within this story. One is a creation story, told in service to Jesus' glory. The other is a gospel story, told in service to our belief. "This, the first of his signs, Jesus did at Cana in Galilee, and manifested his glory. And his disciples believed in him" (2:11).

To hear the creation story, think back to John's famous prologue in chapter 1. Once upon a time there was a beginning: "In the beginning was the Word, and the Word was with God, and the Word was God . . . And the Word became flesh and dwelt among us, and we have seen his glory, glory as of the only Son from the Father, full of grace and truth" (1:1, 14).

John's Gospel is a kind of New Testament Genesis. It is "Genesis elaborated, personalized, and grounded in a recognizable geography and history . . . Everything that comes into view

4. Zacharias, *Jesus Among*, 80–81.

in Genesis 1–2 is lived out in the person of Jesus among men and women like us and under the conditions . . . in which we live. The word that gives precision to this comprehensive revelation of God in human form, living (not merely admiring or discussing) the creation, is *incarnation*."[5]

The creator of all that exists was walking again in the cool of the day, not in Eden but Cana. As the glory of God in flesh, Jesus had ultimate creative abilities. Glory is a major emphasis in John's Gospel.[6] Even Jesus' enemies conceded he had immense, unparalleled creative power like no one they had ever seen. But they denied his glory, and thus he would suffer at their hands.

How Jesus' death is part of his glory we'll come to later. For now, we want to see what John saw when Jesus turned water into wine. John saw Jesus' glory. That means his creativity with the water in Cana was an echo of his Genesis creativity. Genesis 1–2 gives us the reverberating *good* and *very good* of "an infinite artist, a Creator in love with his craft."[7] Turning water into wine at the wedding feast was not *ex nihilo* creation, but was apiece with it, because the miracle at Cana follows, as Andy Crouch observed, the grand pattern of creation: *good, to very good, to glory*.[8]

> Grapes are good—wine is very good. And the best wine? The best wine, for someone prepared by years of observing and tasting and swirling (for all glory requires preparation and skill to be fully recognized), is among the most glorious experiences of which the human senses of sight, taste, and smell are capable. The odd truth is that the most glorious things are the ones that begin as the simplest. A bundle of grapes—the right grapes, at the right time, in the right hands—can become the glory and honor of the nations.[9]

Crouch drew from Revelation 21:26 at the end of his quotation a passage that anticipates the all-things-new fullness of Jesus'

5. Peterson, *Christ Plays*, 86.
6. John 2:11; 7:39; 9:3; 11:4, 40.
7. Wilson, *Notes*, 29.
8. Crouch, *Playing God*, 104.
9. Crouch, *Playing God*, 105–6.

consummate reign from New Jerusalem. The municipal utility there will be Jesus himself: "The city has no need of sun or moon to shine on it, for the glory of God gives it light, and its lamp is the Lamb" (Rev 21:23).

There are no bright lights in John 2. Cana was not a big city. But another utility, water—water specifically reserved for hand- and foot-washing—was transformed. And yet the glory Jesus displayed in the doing of this miracle did not alter his appearance in any way. The power he employed to turn water into wine didn't transfigure him like the time he took three disciples with him up on a mountain to meet Moses and Elijah, "and his face shone like the sun, and his clothes became white as light" (Matt 17:2).

That fits more with what we expect glory to *look* like. It looks like the dazzling light of Jesus that blinded Paul at his conversion.[10] It looks like the experience of Moses when he was granted just a glimpse of God passing by—enough to cause Moses' face to shine for days thereafter, which the people of Israel found more than a little unsettling.[11]

By contrast, the glory displayed by the miracle in Cana was the transformation of a common element, water, by one who continued to look common. The host couldn't believe how great the resulting wine tasted. Wine of astonishment in reverse!

It defied convention to serve the better wine later, after the guests had imbibed enough not to care. The visitation of God's glory at the wedding reception that evening wasn't spectacular in effect, as in old covenant manifestations—like, for instance, in Psalm 29: "He strips the forests bare, and in his temple all cry 'Glory!'" (v. 9)

Jesus came to make the glory of God *approachable* in a way old covenant saints never got to experience. The ones to get the first taste of this were guests at a wedding reception.

> For you have not come to what may be touched, a blazing fire and darkness and gloom and a tempest and the sound of a trumpet and a voice whose words made the

10. Acts 9:1–9.

11. Exod 33:17—34:35; 2 Cor 3:7—4:6.

> hearers beg that no further messages be spoken to them. For they could not endure the order that was given, "If even a beast touches the mountain, it shall be stoned." Indeed, so terrifying was the sight that Moses said, "I tremble with fear." But you have come to Mount Zion and to the city of the living God, the heavenly Jerusalem, and to innumerable angles in festal gathering, and to the assembly of the firstborn who are enrolled in heaven, and to God, the judge of all, and to the spirits of the righteous made perfect, and to Jesus, the mediator of a new covenant."[12]

The difference the gospel makes between the old and new covenants is that *the glory of God becomes approachable in the gospel of Christ*, while giving up nothing for transformative power.

Speaking for my own vocation, I don't think preachers can emphasize the approachableness of God enough. We should not laud the transcendence of God, his *otherness* from us, at the expense of his imminence, his *nearness*. I understand the desire to lift high the name above all names and preach a glorious, big God gospel. But there is a way of "going big" that practically denies what the incarnation is about.

Occasionally I will hear Isaiah 42:8—"I am the Lord; that is my name; my glory I give to no other"—as a zero-sum warning against thinking ourselves too friendly with God. A friend of mine calls this doing touchdown dances on the 50-yard-line. He means when we *only* emphasize a high, holy attribute of God, we think we're defending God's honor, but we may be succeeding only in alienating people from the Lord, who has drawn near to us. We're not giving the whole picture.

> So what does God mean when he says, "My glory I give to no other" in Isaiah 42:8? The answer is in the second phrase of the poetic couplet, "nor my praise to idols." God is unwilling to give his glory *to other would-be gods*. What makes the Creator God jealous is precisely those false gods that share none of their glory, that rob image bearers of their intended glory and dominion over God's

12. Heb 12:18–24.

> very good world, and that remake God's image bearers in their own image, turning us into greedy exploiters of one another and the whole creation for our doomed projects of self-glorification. These false gods are nothing like the true Creator God, who intended from the beginning to pour out glory and honor on his own image bearers. In fact, what distinguishes the true God from every idol is precisely *his generosity with glory*; for it is this Creator's desire that the earth be filled with glory, refracted through the dominion of his image bearers, fruitful and multiplying until there is nowhere where the true God is not named and known.[13]

## Generously Lavish

The point of the incarnation was to draw near to us. Would it be even too much to say that the point was to party with us? This takes us to the gospel story told in service to our belief. I love how the late Brennan Manning wrote about it in *The Ragamuffin Gospel*: "it is unimaginable to picture a wooden faced, stoic, joyless, and judgmental Jesus as he reclined with ragamuffins. The human personality of Jesus is underrated when it is perceived as a passive mask for the dramatic speeches of divinity. Such timidity robs Jesus of his humanity . . . and concludes that he neither laughed, cried, smiled, nor got hurt but simply passed through our world without emotional engagement."[14]

No indeed! "The Word became flesh and blood and moved into the neighborhood," as *The Message* puts John 1:14. The gospel is that the glory of God is not just seen by us in the face of Jesus, but shared with us by Jesus in our actual life experiences. "We saw the glory with our own eyes, the one-of-a-kind glory, like Father, like Son, generous inside and out, true from start to finish."

Let's linger on the generosity. Wine aficionados talk about a wine's finish. They key on the tannins and whether a wine is "fruit-forward." A long finish means the aftertaste stays on the palate.

13. Crouch, *Playing God*, 99–100.

14. Manning, *Ragamuffin*, 61.

That night in Cana, the wine had a generously long finish in spiritual effect. We're still talking about it. Being the first of Jesus' signs, it was a fruit-forward miracle. More generosity would follow.

In the miracles John showcases, water turns to wine, the lame walk, blind people see, dead men rise. These are all acts of creative power personally eyewitnessed by John. Later in the book of Acts, when John witnessed Peter call a lame man onto his feet, the miracle was powered by Jesus. His power did not die with him.[15]

Jesus spent God's creative power lavishly and inexhaustibly. The gospel is wondrous and wonder-working because it follows the pattern of good to very good to glory, set into creation long ago by the same Creator who stretched out the firmament above. Centuries later I picture him stretching his legs on a cushion in a corner of that crowded house in Cana. He motions at his disciples with a wink and a head nod: *Look at the servants. They can't believe they're about to do this!*

Wash-pot water. Star-bright wine. How?

Another Bridegroom was at the Cana wedding. Jesus didn't have to do anything miraculous there. He said as much to his mother, with whom he wasn't being curt when he said that his actions would be in view of the hour ahead of him from now on—that hour being his death on the cross. That would be his ultimate act of creative generosity, the reason he came.

John is like a gospel sommelier. He carefully selected from all he saw and heard about this wedding story to begin his tale. For years, I read this story and completely missed the gospel in it. Jesus' glory is "not primarily about the glitter and the glow of the supernatural."[16] It is primarily about *the hour* that would come for Jesus when he would be lifted up on a cross, generously pour out his blood like wine, and rise from death on the third day.

Take a step back with me here to see this. It seems almost jarring for John to move from the wedding in Cana to the temple cleansing in Jerusalem at the end of chapter 2. But this was quite strategic. John arranged his material more theologically

15. Acts 3:1–10.

16. George, "Waiting," para. 11.

than chronologically. When Jesus was asked for a sign to validate just who he thought he was, he pointed to his coming death and resurrection:

> "What sign do you show us for doing these things?" Jesus answered them, "Destroy this temple, and in three days I will raise it up." . . . He was speaking about the temple of his body. (2:18–19, 21)
>
> "No one has ascended into heaven except he who descended from heaven, the Son of Man. And as Moses lifted up the serpent in the wilderness, so must the Son of Man be lifted up, that whoever believes in him may have eternal life." (3:13–15)
>
> And Jesus answered them, "The hour has come for the Son of Man to be glorified . . . And I, when I am lifted up from the earth, will draw all people to myself." He said this to show by what kind of death he was going to die. (12:23, 32–33)

All this is in view from the wedding feast story. John wants us to keep the bigger picture in mind.

John tells us that Jesus went to the wedding feast on a *third day* (v. 1). He makes mention there of his *hour* (v. 4). Through the transformative miracle, Jesus manifests his *glory* and the disciples *believe* (v. 11).

What's the bigger picture? The gospel. There's no cross yet in John 2:1–11. But there is signaling of its coming and effect in certain phrases Jesus used: *third day*, *my hour*, *manifest glory*, and *they believed*. His coming hour was what everyone associated with him would have to use to keep time from then on.

Mary turned to Jesus when the wine ran out on the wedding party. *You need to do something about this,* she said. And Jesus would. He wouldn't let the party die. He replenished the wine. But he also signaled that he would do more than she or anyone else anticipated: he would let himself die when his hour came.

No one could get the full import of that then, but Mary nonetheless responded to her son with trust. She directed the servants to do whatever Jesus told them.

John saw in Jesus a local Galilean for whom nothing was too difficult.[17] He did powerfully creative things with common elements, and generously. He did what was good and very good, just like at the outset of creation. He may have been from Nazareth, but he was clearly otherworldly. Jesus personified the glory of the Creator in power, full of grace and truth.

## When the Wine Runs Out

Some things in life are genuinely heartbreaking. The sorrow of longings unfulfilled. Personal tragedies. Terminal diagnoses. I remember hearing a well-known theologian talk about how he and his wife had taken relational inventory of their friend network. They realized no one they knew who loved Jesus deeply had not been marked by some kind of intense suffering. The wine runs out us on all.

Jesus enters those places in the miracle stories. Christianity has more to say about human disappointment and suffering than every other religion or philosophy, because only the Christian God has wounds. Years ago, someone highlighted for me that line in Isaiah 53 about Jesus bearing our sorrows.[18] I knew he bore my sin, but it was a personal and pastoral watershed for me to see him bearing my sorrows, too.

Later on, something else in Isaiah also popped off the page. It's the last verse in Isaiah 35, where the prophet anticipates "the ransomed of the Lord" returning to Zion "with singing . . . and sorrow and sighing shall flee away" (v. 10). I remembered a couple of occasions where Jesus is said to have sighed—at least one of those times in response to people seeking signs from him.[19] Jesus' own sorrow will be on display later outside Lazarus's tomb.

The wedding party in Cana running short on wine is on the Sighing side of the Sorrow-to-Sighing continuum. The one

17. Jer 32:17.

18. Isa 53:3–4.

19. Mark 7:34; 8:12.

responsible for the wine order probably wished for a Right to Be Forgotten law when his mistake was revealed. Social custom in a shame-honor culture comes down like a sledgehammer on anyone who cannot provide for guests.

No one was going to die for a depleted wine stock, however. In the miracle stories that follow, we find sick children, blind beggars, and the death of dear friends. That's all firmly on the Sorrow side.

We get a sense of a sigh in Jesus' response to his mother's prodding, "They have no wine." And he said, "What does this have to do with me?" I don't hear sharp rebuke in that. More like sighing. When my wife sighs to our children *your clothes are on the floor*, they know she's not making an observation so much as she is stating a (frustrated) expectation: own your mess and pick up your clothes.

When Jesus said "What does this have to do with me?" he knew he was going to do something about the wine. He would rescue the party. And it seems that most guests in the moment were totally unaware of the miracle. But he wouldn't be coerced into action. Not even by his mother.

He was working for his Father. He would powerfully do this miracle for his mother and for the wedding host and guests and disciples that night—and do more and greater besides, all the way down through time for you and me now. With God in our midst, more is happening than we know.

There are times we *need* to sigh, and times we *need* the sorrows. The world is not yet put to rights. Paul refers to it as groaning:

> For we know that the whole creation has been groaning together as in the pains of childbirth until now. And not only the creation, but we ourselves, who have the firstfruits of the Spirit, groan inwardly as we wait eagerly for adoption as sons, the redemption of our bodies. For in this hope we were saved. Now hope that is seen is not hope. For who hopes for what he sees? But if we hope for what we do not see, we wait for it with patience. (Rom 8:22–25)

What are we waiting for? Another wedding feast. I wonder if John thought back to the night in Cana when he recorded in Revelation that an angel told him to write: "Blessed are those who are invited to the marriage supper of the Lamb" (19:9). The folks in ancient Cana got the first taste of God's glory made approachable. We'll get the last. Another Bridegroom. Another wedding feast. Not in Cana, but New Jerusalem.

Then and only then is when everything finally comes together for us. Then and only then is when our transformation from one degree of glory to another will be complete. Things may be fine for now. Things may be even great and improving for us. But then and only then is when our faith becomes, finally and fully, sight. Then and only then are we living the dream.

The miracle of redemption restores the work of creation and repairs everything sin damaged. Who better to do that work than the Creator himself? We await a wedding feast even now, where the glory and honor of the nations will be taken into the heavenly city, where the marriage supper of the Lamb is served. Isaiah 60 seems to indicate that the cultural fruits of commerce, industry, technology, and agriculture will be in some way purified by God and reclaimed and renewed by him when his kingdom comes in power. Why not viticulture too? No longer will wine astonish for the way too much of it makes one stagger. There will never again be such a thing as too much wine.

Maybe what comes up from New Jerusalem's wine cellars will be that old Cana vintage. I can't wait for a glass.

## John 4:46–54, ESV

So he came again to Cana in Galilee, where he had made the water
wine. And at Capernaum there was an official whose son was ill. 47
When this man heard that Jesus had come from Judea to Galilee,
he went to him and asked him to come down and heal his son, for
he was at the point of death. 48 So Jesus said to him, "Unless you
see signs and wonders you will not believe." 49 The official said
to him, "Sir, come down before my child dies." 50 Jesus said to
him, "Go; your son will live." The man believed the word that Jesus
spoke to him and went on his way. 51 As he was going down, his
servants met him and told him that his son was recovering. 52 So
he asked them the hour when he began to get better, and they said
to him, "Yesterday at the seventh hour the fever left him." 53 The
father knew that was the hour when Jesus had said to him, "Your
son will live." And he himself believed, and all his household. 54
This was now the second sign that Jesus did when he had come
from Judea to Galilee.

# 2

# Believing Is Seeing

Consciousness feels like a miracle. The constellation of these impulses we call love feels like a miracle. The miracles do not cancel out evil, but I accept evil in order to participate in the miraculous.

—David Sheff[1]

I've presided over the funerals of three children in a quarter century of ministry. Even so, three is too high a number. In a ranking of things I care not to repeat, a child's funeral is number one.

For most of history, people agonized over whether their children would live. The benefit of our living now in an era of vaccinations, improved nutrition, and advanced medical practices makes for fewer childhood fatalities from illness. It happens still, but in the centuries leading up to this one, almost every family suffered through the deaths of children, often more than once.

Take James Garfield as representative, our twentieth president. His term of service did not reach a full year before his assassination. Sepsis killed President Garfield due to unsanitary

1. Sheff, *Beautiful Boy*, 250.

medical practices. The assassin's bullet would have been cleanly extracted had he lived in our era. But preceding his own tragic death, Garfield had to grieve the loss of two of his children:

> At his home in Washington, he watched helplessly as his youngest child, Neddie, a beautiful little boy who had contracted whooping cough . . . died in his small bed. After he had lost Trot [his daughter Eliza], so many years earlier, Garfield had thought he could never again feel such an all-consuming sorrow. He realized now how wrong he had been . . . Despite his belief in the goodness of God, Garfield knew that death was cruel, unpredictable, and, too often, unpreventable . . . Searching for a way to teach his children this hard truth, to prepare them for what inevitably lay ahead, Garfield had often turned to what he knew best—books. After dinner one evening, he pulled a copy of Shakespeare's *Othello* off the shelf and began to read the tragedy aloud. "The children were not pleased with the way the story came out," he admitted in his diary, but he hoped that they would come to "appreciate stories that [do not] come out well, for they are very much like a good deal of life."[2]

Garfield was imparting to his surviving children a wisdom that increases sorrow, as the Preacher in Ecclesiastes puts it.[3] And like President Garfield's children, we also are none too pleased with the ways tragedies go. We ache for those cast in a role they did not audition for.

When writer Ann Hood's five-year-old daughter, Grace, died suddenly from a virulent form of strep throat, the Hoods plunged into the deep end of grief, with no clear horizon for orientation. "Grief is not linear. People kept telling me that once this happened or that passed, everything would be better. Some people gave me one year to grieve. They saw grief as a straight line, with a beginning, a middle, and an end. But it is not linear. It is disjointed . . . It

2. Millard, *Destiny*, 17.

3. Eccl 1:18.

is hours that are all right, and weeks that aren't. Or it is good days and bad days."[4]

The grief Hood described can compound. Marriages sometimes do not survive the death of a child. Like black holes that develop in space when stars collapse in on themselves, the gravity of searing loss extinguishes lightness of being. To quote the Preacher in Ecclesiastes again:

> Remember also your Creator in the days of your youth, before the evil days come and the years draw near of which you say, "I have no pleasure in them"; before the sun and the light and the moon and the stars are darkened, and the clouds return after the rain, in the day when the keepers of the house tremble, and the strong men are bent, and the grinders cease because they are few, and those who look through the windows are dimmed. (Eccl 12:1–3)

## Results May Vary

I think those words in Ecclesiastes fitly describe the pall hanging over a house in which a child lays dying. Evil days. Darkened stars. Trembling household. People are living in the basement of their feelings. Into a stark place like that, Jesus—*remember also your Creator*—sent his second sign.

The Capernaum family on the receiving end of Jesus' healing grace was an indirect beneficiary. It's not that they play a bit part in the drama. It's that the miracle, while being for the sick boy, was not about him. His family got something from Jesus many others did not. Jesus' signs and wonders were about revealing his glory to everyone (he's the Creator in flesh with power), and for validating anyone's belief in him (he's the Savior full of grace and truth).

We feel a tension here, however. Why does God not do for all what he does for some? Weren't there other sick children near death in a community the size of Capernaum? Could another

4. Hood, *Comfort*, 52–53.

anxious father have been out searching for Jesus but never found him?

We know from the Gospels that the human misery index was rather high everywhere Jesus went, and that desperate people were always seeking him out to do something for them. The people in his time knew that covenant curses from Deuteronomy were in effect. But Jesus was also doing things an old description said one who would lift the curse would do: "Then the eyes of the blind shall be opened, and the ears of the deaf unstopped; then shall the lame man leap like a deer, and the tongue of the mute sing for joy" (Isa 35:5–6).

We seek these things from Jesus still. I know parents seeking out Jesus to heal kids who've made themselves sick on drugs and alcohol abuse. One mother told me she couldn't abide one more story of God breaking the bonds of addiction for other people's children with hers still in that plight. Deliverance testimonies didn't inflate her hopes, but stoked her fears: *Will my child ever be whole again? And if not, why?*

Those who challenge God's existence or personal goodness sometimes vent that miraculous selectivity on his part is patently unfair. Would to God that all sons and daughters in need of any kind of healing got it! But if God doesn't heal everybody, it doesn't follow that he is not allowed to heal anybody. If there is a God above us revealing his infinite glory, his actions are, in the end and along the way, not fully knowable.

This is not entirely emotionally satisfying. Putting it this way is not meant to shut every mouth before it opens to form pointed questions for God. That God teaches us lament in Scripture means he knows we need to work through our hard questions. It is arduous work. Consider Seth Haines's experience, from his memoir *Coming Clean*:

> I remember the mornings at Children's Hospital. There, Titus and I stood on the fifth-floor window, on a walk down the hall, watching the morning rush on the highway below. I hold this memory: his cheek framed by the feeding tube that runs up his nose and down into his

> intestines . . . I take hold of the pole to which Titus's IV, feeding pump, feeding bag, and tube are attached, and walk back toward our room . . . My phone rings . . . It is a churchman, who says, "I'd like to share a bit of hope with you." He shares the story of his own sick son, how he was also once wasting away. He shares how God provided miraculous salvation by way of faith. He pauses, says, "God orchestrated everything to achieve his ultimate glory. God will bring you an answer in good time because you are a man of faith." He means all the hope in the world, but I feel gut punched. He's wrong. I'm not a man of faith these days. I've converted to a fraud. I've given up on prayer . . . In the days following, others will call, tell me that God ordained this moment in his sovereignty to bring himself glory. Their theology is painful. I cannot see my son as a pawn in God's grand glory-hoarding scheme. It is too much.[5]

We feel tension here also. We don't need to try and preserve the goodness of God at the expense of his sovereignty. God is not "glory-hoarding." It is as much an error to say God has nothing to do with a child's illness as to say anything is outside God's control. But what Haines was looking for was permission to lament and grieve, to vent the questions lodged deep in his spirit. God's glory includes his being big enough to take them. That was being denied him by those who sought to minister out of a kind of linearism, as well as bad timing.

> An expert on death and dying reports an incident many of us will understand. A woman came out of a sickroom where a loved one was dying and asked in a tightly controlled voice, "Is there a room anywhere in the hospital where I can go to scream?" A doctor directed her to a place and later mused over the idea that every hospital—maybe every office and home [and church community]—ought to have a screaming room.[6]

5. Haines, *Coming Clean*, 82–84.

6. Plantinga, *Beyond Doubt*, 28.

## The Journey in Believing

Perhaps a screaming room was needed in Capernaum of old. There a boy lay dying in his bed. Labored breathing. Spiking fever.

His parents felt helpless, because they were. No IV drips back then. No feeding tubes. No children's hospitals. The fact that people in earlier times were more accustomed to deaths of children did not make it any easier for them to endure. The flowers in the garden were not grown in anticipation of decorating the funeral bier of their son. In any era, a sick child turns a house too quiet. It is the explosive silence of people living on edge.

The boy's dad was a local official, likely a Herod appointee rather than Roman, meaning he was the kind of man people wanted to do things for, being no sellout to Rome. He learned Jesus was back in Galilee. To pinpoint it, Jesus was back in the town of Cana, where he turned the water into wine. That was about a day's walk from Capernaum.

Hope broke through clouds and burned away the fog of inertia. He would go to Jesus in Cana, get him to journey home with him, and heal his son. Flannery O'Connor, afflicted with lupus, once wrote that being sick was like visiting another country where eventually you find you've taken up residence.[7] The man wouldn't have to leave his home region to get to Jesus, but he was more than ready to move out of the far country of consuming illness.

But when he located Jesus, he found him kind of surly: "Unless you see signs and wonders you will not believe," Jesus said (v. 48). Or maybe sighed? Why?

Jesus was ambivalent about the citizenry in his native region. For good reason: they tended to be dismissive of him by heritage. The old-timers remembered him as a boy. He'd waited on them in Joseph's carpentry business. They knew his siblings' opinions of him.[8]

7. "I have never been anywhere but sick. In a sense sickness is a place, more instructive than a long trip to Europe, and it's always a place where there's no company, where nobody can follow" (quoted in Elie, *Life You Save*, 282).

8. Mark 3:21; John 7:5.

John says in verse 45 that the Galileans welcomed him because there was no doubt he could do incredible things. But in verse 44, just before that report, John repeats an adage about a prophet being without honor in his hometown. How does one honor a prophet? *Believe* him. All through the Old Testament, up to John the Baptist in the New Testament, the way to honor a prophet as someone sent from God was to believe and do what the prophet said God wanted.

Think about that time Jesus told the religious authorities to call their bet on John the Baptist. Was he a prophet sent to them by God, or not? If they agreed he was, they knew Jesus would immediately counter with, "Then why didn't you believe him?" (Matt 21:25). Jesus preached a message of repentance and belief. So did the apostles after him: "But to all who did receive him, who believed in his name, he gave the right to become children of God" (John 1:12). "But these are written so that you may believe that Jesus is the Christ, the Son of God, and that by believing you may have life in his name" (John 20:31).

In public access, belief is something of a turnstile word. It designates whatever people find meaningful (I believe in love) or factual (I believe in science) or possible ("Believe!" signs on an underdog's home field). For most people, beliefs are extensions of their personal feelings and opinions, as well as what they think they know or wish to be true.

In Scripture, belief begins with believing the truth about Jesus and then develops into being true to Jesus. Belief is the ground floor in allegiance. Faith is trusting in what we have good reason to believe is true.[9] John ties our good reasons to Jesus' signs. His signs lead us somewhere: to identify Jesus with God.

Gospel belief is not the true-to-yourself messaging that dominates Western culture. Think of most every princess movie you've seen (I'm the dad of three girls). The messaging is to always believe in yourself, be true to yourself, and never give up on your dreams. But "suppose the 'self' to which we are to be true is the self that wants to cheat everyone you meet, including friends and family,

9. Koukl, *Story of Reality*, 137.

out of as much money as possible?"[10] No princess ever wanted that for anyone, of course. But most believe-in-yourself messaging assumes whatever we find within ourselves is right and true and we should go with it. It assumes we *will* find truth in ourselves eventually if we just keep looking. Shakespeare would be surprised to see that we've turned his Polonius character ("To thine own self be true")—whom he called "a foolish prating knave"—into something of a standard-bearer.

> How, in a relatively short period of time, did we go from a world where belief in God was the default assumption to our secular age in which belief in God seems, to many, unbelievable? This brave new world is not just the old world with the God-supplement lopped off; it's not just the world that is left when we subtract the supernatural. A secular world where we have permission, even encouragement, to *not* believe in God is an accomplishment, not merely a remainder. Our secular age is the product of creative new options, an entire reconfiguration of meaning . . . [It's] not that our secular age is an age of *dis*belief; it's an age of believing otherwise.[11]

Being true to Jesus, as he has revealed himself to us in Scripture, is the point and purpose in Christian belief. But it's not about the journey so much as the destination. It begins when we recognize who Jesus is and that he lived the life we should have lived (perfection in God's will and way) but wouldn't because of our sin. If one needs cinching signs to identify Jesus with God, fine. Jesus did many signs and wonders while preaching faith and repentance. But being true to Jesus is the fruit of repentance in action, the ongoing formation of his virtues in us.

What about doubt? Is there room for doubt in believing in Jesus? The father in John 4 doesn't seem to grapple with doubt. He takes Jesus at his word and gets what he came to Jesus for. But even some who received the Great Commission *in person* doubted.[12]

10. Wright, *After You Believe*, 51.
11. Smith, *How Not to Be Secular*, 47.
12. Matt 28:17.

And John includes the account of Thomas, to whom Jesus said post-resurrection, "Have you believed because you have seen me? Blessed are those who have not seen and yet have believed" (20:29).

Among them are Christians who battle doubts of varying intensities. To recognize this doesn't automatically commit the error of the minister in the novel *A Prayer for Owen Meany*—Reverend Merrill—who preached that doubt was the essence, not the opposite, of faith.[13] Blessing doubt like that is a disservice to the people of God, an example of feet firmly planted in midair.

Belief has to land somewhere. It may not always land smoothly. There are cultural crosswinds to contend with in this.

> Because the broader culture treats doubt as the apex of our intellectual experience, there are cultural incentives for those who embrace it. For young, culturally cosmopolitan evangelical Christians, the cultural rewards are all on the side of tossing out the truths we've inherited and starting again from the beginning. Trafficking in doubt draws a crowd, as anxious uncertainty strikes us as more authentic and courageous than firm conviction. It is bold to ask our questions, we think, and cowardly to retreat to the creed.[14]

In other words, we now grant the benefit of the doubt to the doubter being true to his doubts. He is just being honest, we say. But our questioning is not always honest, nor is it neutral. License to doubt freely may harbor hostility toward God. There can be places in us where repentance has yet to reach. Couple with this our capacity for self-deception. In this vein, I appreciate how the poet Christian Wiman deals with doubting in his book *My Bright Abyss*:

> You know the value of your doubt by the quality of the disquiet that it produces in you. Is it a furious, centrifugal sort of anxiety that feeds on itself and never seems to move you in any one direction? Is it an ironclad compulsion to refute, to find in even the most transfiguring experiences, your own or others', some rational

13. Irving, *Prayer for Owen Meany*, 550.

14. Anderson, *End*, 49.

> or "psychological" explanation? Is it an almost religious commitment to doubt itself, an assuredness that absolute doubt is the highest form of faith? There is something static and self-enthralled about all these attitudes. Honest doubt, what I would call devotional doubt, is marked, it seems to me, by three qualities: humility, which makes one's attitude impossible to celebrate; insufficiency, which makes it impossible to rest; and mystery, which continues to tug you upward—or at least outward—even in your lowest moments. Such doubt is painful—more painful, in fact, than any of the other forms—but its pain is active rather than passive, purifying rather than stultifying. Far beneath it, no matter how severe its drought, how thoroughly your skepticism seems to have salted the ground of your soul, faith, durable faith, is steadily taking root.[15]

As Chaucer put it, believers are endeavoring to own God's ownership of us:

> This life so short, this craft so long to learn. Our understanding of God, of ourselves, and of the world comes so slowly, so painfully slowly, that life's summer passes and the winter arrives long before this fruit is ripe to be picked. Or so it seems. But God is not a quantity that can be mastered even though he can be known; and though he has revealed himself with clarity, the depth of our understanding of him is measured, not by the speed with which theological knowledge is processed, but by the quality of our determination to own his ownership of us through Christ.[16]

John would have liked that way of putting it, I think. A believer is someone being true to how Jesus revealed himself to be God in flesh, and true to what he wants from us, which is for us to take him at his word. Owning his ownership of us.

15. Wiman, *My Bright Abyss*, 75–76.

16. Quoted in Wells, "Theologian's Craft," 173.

## There and Back Again

The miracles preached belief and believing. More to the point, they were gospel sign language directed at a particular kind of cultural deafness. Galileans thought they listened to God and heard from God. But did they?

It wasn't hard for the homefolks to listen to Jesus preach repentant faith. All prophets sermonized on that theme. What was hard for them was to hear Jesus make *himself* the recipient of their repentant faith. It was hard for those he grew up among to believe what he was saying about himself, though they clearly saw, and sought, application of his power to their problems.

But the Galilean father in John 4, seeking a brother Galilean's help—he hears Jesus criticize the need for signs, then affirm why he did them in the same breath: "Unless you see signs and wonders you will not believe" (v. 48). In reply the man, whom John is careful to remind us is an official, tries to leverage every bit of his social standing to see his son well again. "Sir, come down before my child dies" (v. 49).

The gist of that statement is this: *I don't really care about signs, just heal my son!*[17] He walked for hours and already asked once (v. 47), only to hear Jesus come back at him like a kind of stickler parliamentarian standing on an obscure point of order. It brought to mind for me a time when I once called my congressman, years ago, to urge him to vote for a bill that included protections for the religiously persecuted in ally nations. During our brief interaction, I felt completely patronized by him. He somehow maneuvered our conversation from his supporting the bill to my church supporting him.

Jesus wasn't oily like that, but here with the official, he did make it about himself. How come? The question was never whether Jesus could do unbelievable things for people, but why people needed the unbelievable done in order to believe in him. What is it about hardness of heart that requires supernatural interference

17. Peterson, *Christ Plays*, 94.

to move us off unbelief? Why was the word of prophets, and Jesus' own words, not enough?

As if on cue, the official brought it back to his son, to the immediate urgent need. And Jesus did precisely what the man wanted him to do. But the way he did it was to speak it into being: "Go, your son will live" (v. 50).

God's speaking is his acting. His word creates. The official, knowing Jesus wasn't going down to Capernaum with him, took Jesus at his word and went back to find a boy who could again run out to greet his father's homecoming.

Of all the miracle stories John says he had to choose from, why this one? It is a feat of precision molecular marksmanship from miles away. And it is touching, too. Who doesn't want to see a sick little boy well? In healing the boy, we see Jesus wed his power to his compassion, and we see that he was no respecter of persons. He served the rich and the poor, the down-and-out and the up-and-out. But this is not chiefly why John chose this story for his record.

He chose this one because the situation the man from Capernaum found himself in parallels our own. To believe the Bible, to affirm it as the word of God, means accepting the historicity of biblical accounts based on the reliability of those living at the time. They wrote down what they personally saw, like John (or like Luke, who wrote what he learned in researching the notes and memories of eye-witnesses[18]).

In this father, we have our own situation downstream in that the man didn't actually witness the wonder of his son's healing. He had to take Jesus at his word and act on what Jesus told him. This we now call saving faith. This is what it means for us to believe the gospel. Blessed are those who have not seen and yet believe.

18. See Luke 1:1–4 and Acts 1:1.

## The Hardest Steps

This story parallels for us what it means to believe in the gospel of Christ in at least two ways: how saving faith trusts in advance for what makes sense in reverse, and how saving faith finds a greater outcome than just a met objective.

Trusting in advance for what will make sense in reverse is a turn of phrase I got from Philip Yancey.[19] He suggests we learn to take the longer view and recognize that in Christ every scar, every hurt, every doubt of ours will eventually be seen in a different light if we stay with Jesus to the end. Everything sad is going to come untrue.[20] So our faith trusts in advance for what will make sense to us then. The miracle in John 4 anticipates this for us.

Most of us are far more in the moment than we realize. If God is performing to our satisfaction right now, we worship him; if he doesn't, why bother? "Ancient people were arguably much more acquainted with brutality, loss, and evil than we are . . . Yet there is virtually no ancient thinker who reasoned from such evil that, therefore, there couldn't be a God."[21] But we moderns reason this way all the time.

The miracles of Jesus didn't address every human disappointment. And as we'll see in chapters 3 and 6, miracles made little difference to anyone determined to deny that Jesus was the Son of God. But this particular miracle in John 4 was no *I'll believe it when I see it*. The seeing *followed* the believing.

> In all my life I have met only one person who claims to have seen a ghost. And the interesting thing about the story is that that person disbelieved in the immortal soul before she saw the ghost and still disbelieves after seeing it. She says that what she saw must have been an illusion or a trick of the nerves. And obviously she may be right. Seeing is not believing.[22]

19. Yancey, *Finding God*, 178.
20. Tolkien, *Return of the King*, 930.
21. Keller, *Making Sense*, 37.
22. Lewis, *Miracles*, 205.

There are people who tell us they cannot believe in God because they've never seen him. The assumption is that if he would show himself to them, they would believe, for then he would prove his existence. It is commonly thought that something does not count as real knowledge unless there is empirical proof of it. But very few of our beliefs actually require mathematical or scientific verification. How does one do laboratory tests to prove his love for his mother, or reproduce in a petri dish the existence of the presidency of James Garfield? How does one even prove that knowledge has to be provable?

If we had lived at the right time in history, in first-century Galilee, we would have seen God with our own eyes in Jesus. But we still would have had to take him at his word. Seeing was no guarantee of believing back then either. Many did see Jesus, but did not believe in him.

"Some things just have to be believed to be seen."[23] This is how faith in the gospel of Christ works. When you and I believe in Jesus through the gospel message of God's grace for our sin, we trust in advance that what we're doing will make sense in reverse.

What did the official in our story, a man in charge of things, see? He saw that Jesus was way more in charge of things than he'd ever been. He saw that taking Jesus at his word was more than worthwhile. But the hardest step of the day had to be turning for home, knowing that Jesus wouldn't go with him. Jesus sent him back home with only his word to go on. He had to trust in advance that that would make sense in reverse when he played it back through later.

One of my favorite movies is *The Secret Life of Walter Mitty*. Walter Mitty, played by Ben Stiller, handles negatives acquisition (film rolls) for *Life Magazine*. It's technical work, predictable and steady, and an extension of his routinized personality.

Walter Mitty is forced by circumstances to hunt down an intrepid photographer who does nothing but take risky assignments. He discovers that the man is in Greenland. Mitty gets there

23. Yancey, *Disappointment with God*, 130.

to learn that he just missed him; the photographer boarded a ship ported there the day before, sailing for Iceland.

The only way Walter Mitty can get to that ship is to catch a ride with a drunk helicopter pilot flying radio parts to it. He knows it's crazy to go with the guy, but it's his only chance. He *has to* get to the photographer. As he deliberates with himself, he imagines the girl he's in love with back home. He imagines her on the karaoke stage. She's singing David Bowie's "Ground Control to Major Tom," a song about facing your fears and taking courage.

Suddenly, Mitty gets up from the table and turns to the exit door. That's the hardest step. He runs outside to the helicopter, clutching his briefcase to his chest. Just as it lifts from the ground he leaps in, his face awash in disbelief that he did it. But there was nothing else he could do if he was going to catch up to his photographer. He had to act.

"Go; your son will live" (v. 50). Many think conversion to Christ means missing out on so much you would otherwise experience. But in the ultimate consideration of things, it will prove worth it to have believed in Jesus in this world, even if we miss out on some things that look great from a distance—and even if we don't get some of the things we want from him.

The greater tragedy is God not getting what he wants from us. The Capernaum official with the sick son wanted something from God and got it. But God also wanted something from him. The guy standing before Jesus in John 4 is standing in for us all in this way: Jesus wants people to take him at his word. That's the choice before us. Will we? It's what believing the gospel requires at the start and all the way through.

This second sign event shows us the hardest step, which is not going out the door and up the road to find Jesus and dare make a request of him. We do that all the time. It's practically considered a constitutional right by most Americans to ask God for whatever we want whenever we want it, whether we believe in him or not.

The harder step is when we have nothing more than his word to go on: *Go. Take me at my word. Follow through.* That might put us out of step or out of sorts with the world around us, or even with our own desires. To take Jesus at his word in a fallen world creates all kinds of tensions and struggles for us. But that's the kind of belief Jesus wants from believers: belief that will advance our trust in him, come what may.

Jesus was a son too. God's Son would eventually go back down to Judea. There he would be betrayed and humiliated and killed. Why? Because of the official and his son, and his household and staff, and everybody else in Capernaum and Cana; because of everyone in Memphis, where I live; because of everyone else wherever it is you live and beyond. Jesus would go to the cross because of you and me and all of us.

The official, when greeted by his staff bearing the good news that his boy was well, asked what hour his son began to improve. "Yesterday at the seventh hour the fever left him" (v. 52). That was exactly the hour he was interceding with Jesus for him.

Six hours of suffering on a dark Friday is still ahead of Jesus. By the seventh hour in that story, God's son is dead, drained of life to pay for our sin. That self-sacrifice didn't make sense to anyone at the time. Doesn't it now in reverse?

## All the Way Home

This story inverts the old adage that seeing is believing. But there is a second way this story parallels for us what it means to believe in the gospel of Christ. It has to do with how saving faith finds a greater outcome than just objective met. In this story, the son is restored to health—objective met—but the greater outcome is that the man and his whole household believe in Jesus.

That's a greater outcome, because eventually they would all die: the son, his father and mother, and the household. Everyone. If more life is all we're living for, eventually life runs out on us. The hourglass was overturned on us the day of our births, and the sands don't stop. Life expectancies have increased well beyond the range most ancients knew, but the sands still trickle out on us every day.

Every sign John recorded communicates the gospel story. They're not standalones, but linked as means to the ends of life in his name. Belief is the objective. But life in his name is the greater outcome (cf. 20:30–31).

Principally, life in his name means we get to live on with him beyond our mortal lives. Eternal life is Jesus' own indestructible life gifted to us. It is life beyond the reach of death. Practically, life in his name is staying in earshot of the gospel. We are "prone to wander," in the words of the old hymn, "Come, Thou Fount." Life in his name waits to find out how it will be that even our scars and hurts and doubts will, from an eternal vantage point, make some kind of sense.

Life in Jesus' name is belief *and* believing. Did you notice how John repeatedly mentioned the father's belief? "The man believed the word that Jesus spoke to him"; (v. 50) "And he himself believed, and all his household" (v. 53).

Belief isn't static. He believed and he believed again. Belief begins at a point in time, but continues on in advancing trust. It is in perpetually present tense. Life in Jesus' name begins at belief, but holds greater outcomes for those who keep believing, resiliently taking Jesus at his word.

> Do you get the point? The whole amazing story of Jesus, with all its multiple levels, is given us to be our story as we follow him. This is John's ultimate vision of the nature of Christian discipleship. At the end of chapter 21, after Jesus' strange and beautiful conversation with Peter, he issues that haunting summons: don't think about what I may or may not require of the person standing next to you. Your call is simply to follow me.[24]

24. Wright, *Following Jesus*, 40.

## John 5:1–18, ESV

After this there was a feast of the Jews, and Jesus went up
to Jerusalem.

2 Now there is in Jerusalem by the Sheep Gate a
pool, in Aramaic called Bethesda, which has five roofed
colonnades. 3 In these lay a multitude of invalids—blind,
lame, and paralyzed. 5 One man was there who had been
an invalid for thirty-eight years. 6 When Jesus saw him
lying there and knew that he had already been there a
long time, he said to him, "Do you want to be healed?"
7 The sick man answered him, "Sir, I have no one to put
me into the pool when the water is stirred up, and while
I am going another steps down before me." 8 Jesus said to
him, "Get up, take up your bed, and walk." 9 And at once
the man was healed, and he took up his bed and walked.

Now that day was the Sabbath. 10 So the Jews said
to the man who had been healed, "It is the Sabbath, and
it is not lawful for you to take up your bed." 11 But he
answered them, "The man who healed me, that man
said to me, 'Take up your bed, and walk.'" 12 They asked
him, "Who is the man who said to you, 'Take up your
bed and walk'?" 13 Now the man who had been healed
did not know who it was, for Jesus had withdrawn, as
there was a crowd in the place. 14 Afterward Jesus found
him in the temple and said to him, "See, you are well!
Sin no more, that nothing worse may happen to you." 15
The man went away and told the Jews that it was Jesus
who had healed him. 16 And this was why the Jews were
persecuting Jesus, because he was doing these things on
the Sabbath. 17 But Jesus answered them, "My Father is
working until now, and I am working."

18 This was why the Jews were seeking all the more
to kill him, because not only was he breaking the Sabbath, but he was even calling God his own Father, making himself equal with God.

# 3

# Disability Check

Some people talk as if meeting the gaze of absolute goodness would be fun. They need to think again.

—C. S. Lewis[1]

Sin no more.

Commands are sent out on the urgent calls, like a kind of verbal ambulance. As commands go, "sin no more" from the mouth of Jesus is for rescuing us from ourselves. It's true what you've heard about yourself being your own worst enemy. Sin, in both unrighteous and self-righteous forms, is like malignant cancer, organically destroying its own host.

Something like this happened to the man Jesus healed in John 5. It's a sin story wrapped within a miracle story. The descriptors of sin are varied throughout the Bible, but the common denominator is personal debilitation:

> The Bible presents sin by way of major concepts, principally lawlessness and faithlessness, expressed in an array of images: sin is the missing of a target, a wandering from the path, a straying from the fold. Sin is a hard heart and

1. Lewis, *Mere Christianity*, 38.

> a stiff neck. Sin is blindness and deafness. It is both the overstepping of a line and the failure to meet it—both transgression and shortcoming . . . Sin is disruption of created harmony and then resistance to divine restoration of that harmony.[2]

That resistance to divine restoration isn't happening outside the church only. As any pastor can tell you, ministry exists because perfect compliance to God's will and ways does not. (The honest pastor finds this resistance in himself also.) Our resistance takes at least two forms: repentance deficit and conviction deficit.

Repentance deficit makes us seem superior to others, like we have no sin ourselves. Conviction deficit makes us accommodate (domesticate) sin. We act as if the disruption of God's created harmony is something he winks at or waves off.

For its punch, I like Francis Spufford's take in his book *Unapologetic*. Written for a skeptical readership, Spufford calls sin "the human propensity to [mess] things up." He formulizes that as "HPtFtU."[3] Spufford's raw definition appropriately conveys the sinfulness of sin.

> What we're talking about here is not just our tendency to lurch and stumble and screw up by accident, our passive role as agents of entropy. It's our active inclination to break stuff, "stuff" here including moods, promises, relationships we care about, and our own well-being as well as other people's, as well as material objects whose high gloss positively seems to invite a big fat scratch.[4]

Repentance deficit denies our ongoing bout with HPtFtU. This is to Sin's advantage. My capitalization of Sin reflects Paul's treatment of it in Romans 7. Sin is portrayed as a Power at work, not just personal accumulation of misdeeds. Sin is a malevolent Power in the world that hijacks even the Law of God and deals Death to humanity.[5] The Power of Sin has to be broken by a greater

2. Plantinga, *Not the Way*, 5.
3. Spufford, *Unapologetic*, 27–28.
4. Spufford, *Unapologetic*, 27.
5. Rutledge, *Crucifixion*, 28, 101.

Power, Christ Jesus himself, whose miracles were each and all displays of his greater Power over the effects of Sin.

Martin Luther famously preached repentance as a way of life: "When our Lord and Master Jesus Christ said, 'Repent,' he willed the entire life of believers to be one of repentance."[6] In Scripture, repentance toward God describes a change of mind, a retooling of our inner motivations. Repentance can also be *away* from God if we change our minds about what God says sin is.

Conviction deficit, by contrast, lacks the fruit of repentance. Repentance is not just turning from things unrighteous. We also need the self-righteousness pulled from us. Repentance returns us to the gospel. Convictions follow. We rise and walk in the direction of Jesus, setting course for a long obedience in the same direction.[7]

Remember *Snow White*? The evil queen disguised herself and presented a poisoned apple. The girl intuited something was up, but then the queen cut the apple in half, eating the good side. That ruse led to Snow's fateful bite into the poisoned half and put her in a death-sleep from which only her prince could rescue her. In its own way, that scene allegorizes Genesis 3. Sin has done the same thing to us. Conviction deficit won't name the queen or her poison, though. Conviction deficit denies sin as the crack in everything that it is.[8] It hedges and dies the death of a thousand qualifications.

I get the term "conviction deficit" from Ross Douthat's book *Bad Religion*, where he describes what he calls accommodationist Christianity:

> In [its] quest to be inclusive and tolerant and up-to-date, the accommodationists imitated [Jesus'] scandalously comprehensive love, while ignoring his scandalously comprehensive judgments. They used his friendship with prostitutes as an excuse to ignore his explicit condemnation of fornication and divorce. They turned his disdain for the religious authorities of his day and his fondness for tax collectors and Roman soldiers into a thin excuse for privileging the secular realm over the sacred. While recognizing his willingness to dine with outcasts and

6. Quoted in Noll, *Turning Points*, 166.
7. Peterson, *Long Obedience*, 13.
8. Spufford, *Unapologetic*, 24.

> converse with nonbelievers, they deemphasized the crucial fact that he had done so in order to heal them and convert them—ridding the leper of his sickness, telling the Samaritans they would *worship in spirit and in truth*, urging the woman taken in adultery to *go, and from now on sin no more*.[9]

The gospel is leveling in that everyone is addressed as a sinner. We should thank God for this. We should rejoice in hearing "sin no more" from his mouth, because God says it to those he wants to work in.

When I started out as a pastor, I once told a mentor how awkward it was to hear someone confess his sin to me. I don't know how I managed to enter the ministry not expecting that, but I didn't know what to say to people in my initial experiences. The wiser pastor said the first thing out of my mouth should be *praise God*. I should welcome confessional conversations because convictions, like seeds, are trying to push up through soil.

## Insiders and Outliers

The third sign event John gives us is Jesus healing a man who suffered paralysis for almost four decades. In the first two signs, the intended effect was realized: belief took root (cf. John 20:30–31; 2:11; 4:50, 53). It appears that the same cannot be said in the third sign event, and I'll give a reason or two why I don't think so.

Think back for a moment on the first sign event: Jesus turned water into wine. Remember how John followed a Genesis creational pattern in telling that story: good, to very good, to glory? This third miracle event, in John 5, almost seems to follow an Exodus story arc. A man is delivered from a long affliction, but remains a kind of "wilderness unto himself."[10]

I wouldn't say that John had an Exodus angle in mind, though John's writings are chock full of Old Testament references and allusions. But in John 5, the man's broken spine is reminiscent of the

9. Douthat, *Bad Religion*, 108.

10. Robinson, *Gilead*, 118–19.

stiff neck and hard heart long characteristic of the old covenant people of God. In verse 18, John gives two main reasons why many in Jesus' time justified resisting him, and later killing him: he broke the Sabbath and made himself equal with God, calling God his own Father.

The culture Jesus negotiated was one of strict monotheism. Sometimes you'll hear people say Jesus never claimed to be God. Not in a direct way, no, because any semblance of walking around saying *Hi, I'm Yahweh* would have been swiftly denounced as blasphemy.

Jesus took a more indirect approach, not because he didn't consider himself divine, but because his society was flooded with expectations for what the messiah had to look like. Chief among those expectations was that he would exercise political power and military might—a liberating conqueror. Jesus often hid himself after doing miracles because he was careful to avoid being pigeonholed by competing messianic narratives. Privately with his disciples he explained everything, as much as they could grasp, but the Gospels mostly record his public interactions.

Those who opposed Jesus saw his work and heard his articulated intimacy with God. He cited himself as his own interpretive authority. He conducted himself with divine exceptionality. There was no category in which to place Jesus other than *so-you-think-you're-God*.

"The Jews," John's shorthand reference for the religious establishment, those who "sat on Moses' seat" (Matt 23:2), were determined to deny Jesus' power as coming from God. They claimed valid theological reasons, but the contempt they showed Jesus, even the violence they breathed out toward him, exposed that it was more about their hardheartedness. Motives are always multiple and frequently mixed.

Culturally, the religious authorities were keen to protect their power. The heightened sense of this was made hyper by Roman occupation. Jews were waiting for a messiah who would kick the Romans out of Jerusalem and return the nation to a Solomonic golden era when no one pushed Israel around. The rabbis were the vanguards of that hope and did not gladly suffer dozens of messianic complexes running around the country. The people, out of an alloy of national loyalty, respect, and personal fear, tended to side with whatever rabbis enforced. Sabbath regulations were kind of like a jurisdiction, and the authorities policed it with the hawkish zeal of deputies itching to issue citations.

Jesus was an outlier in his time. He still is. A certain kind of flair accompanies this in our culture, but there were no cultural rewards for it in Jesus' time. An outlier was an outcast, crossing up the religious establishment's hallowed ways of life. It wasn't the route to success with them.

There were outliers in earnest: people pushed to the margins of community life, often due to their physical afflictions. They were conspicuous in public places—literally out lying around in those places, like at the Bethesda pool in Jerusalem. Under its shady colonnades "lay a multitude of invalids—blind, lame, and paralyzed" (v. 3).

The waters were believed to be medicinal, much like some hot springs are thought to be. The waters were supposed to be at maximum strength when moving. But there was a deflating twist: you had to be the first one in to receive healing.[11] "One man was there who had been an invalid for thirty-eight years" (v. 5). He was a man in need of grace, and truth also. "And the Word became flesh and dwelt among us, and we have seen his glory, glory as of the only Son from the Father, full of grace and truth" (John 1:14).

## Do You Want to be Well?

Jesus held grace and truth in tension in his own person. Grace and truth are good lenses through which to read this story in John 5.

11. There is a textual variant in this story, reflected in how most English translations make verse 4 a footnote: "for an angel of the Lord went down at certain seasons into the pool, and stirred the water: whoever stepped in first after the stirring of the water was healed of whatever disease he had." That could have been what happened at the Bethesda pool, or the waters could have been stirred by underground springs moving, and the legend grew up around hopes invested in that.

In healing the man's broken body, Jesus applied grace. But he also addressed the man's heart through the application of truth meant to break the hold of sin.

The application of Jesus' grace is seen in the act of healing itself, but also in the question preceding it: "Do you want to get well?" (v. 6). To aim at the heart was Jesus' work: "My Father is working until now, and I am working" (v. 17).

His work was to minister grace and truth through the demonstration of creative power over sin, sickness, Satan, and death. That happened spectacularly through his miracles, but also through his preaching and use of Scripture. Jesus was first and foremost a preacher with authority.

Asking a disabled man if he wants to get well strikes many as kind of a stupid question at first blush. It seems like asking the librarian if there are any books to check out of the library. What paralytic *doesn't* want to walk, especially after four long decades of being stepped over (and on)?

Jesus was demonstrating a keen perceptiveness. In Calvin Miller's *The Singer*, the Singer encounters a miller with a deformed hand due to a farming accident suffered years before. The Singer offers to heal him with one of his melodies. But the miller thinks the Singer is mocking him. He thinks the Singer is actually making things worse by calling attention to his gnarled hand. The miller is so full of self-pity he can't recognize the healing agent before him and in fact chases him off.[12]

Rod Dreher wrote appreciatively of the therapist who posed Jesus' diagnostic question to him one day. At first, Dreher couldn't see the relevance to his situation of trying to heal from family dysfunctions. But the therapist was making a point: people who have been suffering something for a long time can actually build their life around it. Even though it is debilitating in so many ways, they are afraid of what freedom from it would mean.[13]

Christian therapists and pastors deal with this dynamic sometimes when addressing the heart. Perceptive questions are

12. Quoted in Brown, *Three Free Sins*, 26.

13. Dreher, *How Dante Can Save*, 192–93.

often the best tool for cutting through evasiveness. We are no more evasive than when we're trying to justify a sin we aren't ready to let go of. Limping along or lying around in the grip of it can become our M.O.

Herman Melville, of *Moby Dick* fame, wrote a short story called "Bartleby, the Scrivener." A scrivener is an antiquated name for a legal copyist. Before the advent of keyboards, he wrote out wills, deeds, and other legal documents longhand.

Set on Wall Street, Bartleby took a small desk beside a window looking out on a brick wall. Soon after starting, he quit, only he never served notice and never left his desk. He just responded to each request made of him with "I would prefer not to," over and over again, staring out his window at the blank brick wall.

Bartleby never left the lawyer's office. He never went home. He appeared to never eat.

The lawyer eventually moved his practice due to his perplexity and distress over how impossible Bartleby turned out to be. Day in and day out, Bartleby stayed at work but did no work. Melville even named his coworkers after food—Turkey, Ginger Nut, and Nippers (lobster)—as if to urge Bartleby to at least eat something. Even in that, Bartleby preferred not to.

The new tenants couldn't make Bartleby leave either, so the police arrested him. They removed Bartleby to a prison cell in the Tombs. There the lawyer visited him, pleading with him again to eat something. Bartleby was wasting away through self-starvation. Still he preferred to just stare at the walls. Returning several days later, the lawyer found Bartleby facing his bleak cell wall, dead.

Bartleby locked himself into what London psychoanalyst Stephen Grosz calls "the grip of negativity." Grosz draws on Melville's story incisively: "The lawyer makes several attempts to coax Bartleby out of his withdrawal, but helping, it turns out, is not so easy. In fact, the story hints at a dark truth: it is the lawyer's help that causes Bartleby's situation to worsen."[14]

The insight fits this third sign event at the Bethesda pool. There is a darker undercurrent in the story. Jesus was nothing but

14. Grosz, *Examined Life*, 126–27.

gracious to the disabled man at the Bethesda pool. Jesus' grace was help. But what did the man do with his healing? Jesus confronted him with "sin no more" later in the temple (v. 14). Jesus was the reason he could walk, but it appears the man preferred not to walk with Jesus.

There is an interpretation of this story that tries to make the man an evangelist; that he runs to tell the Jews that Jesus healed him so they would believe in Jesus, too. While that happens in other accounts of Jesus' healings, I don't think that's what happened here. Neither does Don Carson:

> John's deft portrait of the invalid throughout this chapter paints him in far more dour hues. He tries to avoid difficulties with the authorities by blaming the one who has healed him (v. 11); he is so dull he has not even discovered his benefactor's name (v. 13); once he finds out he reports Jesus to the authorities (v. 15). In this light, verse 7 reads less as an apt and subtle response to Jesus' question than as the crotchety grumblings of an old and not very perceptive man who thinks he is answering a stupid question.[15]

The way John presents this story suggests that all the man did with Jesus' help was become more self-centered. That is the essence of sin. Mobile now, he roamed. Made to stand upright, the man had no real interest in walking uprightly. He preferred not to. It seems he preferred his sin.

## I Prefer Not To

In John 8, Jesus spared a woman caught in adultery the condemnation others wanted to heap upon her. That was grace. He also called her to leave adultery behind her. That was truth. *Go and sin no more.*

In the very next chapter, when Jesus encountered a blind man (chapter 6), his disciples wanted to know if the man's blindness was consequence for some kind of sin—his own or his parents? They were thinking in the old covenant terms they knew, that grief

15. Carson, *Gospel*, 243.

can follow on sin, and Jesus invoked those terms in John 5 when he told this man he met at the Bethesda pool not just to sin no more but added, "that nothing worse may happen to you" (v. 14). In saying that, he was reminding the man of Deuteronomy.

The possibility is at least left open that God afflicted the man as a consequence for something sinful. We don't know this for certain, but according to Deuteronomy 28, disease and other physical afflictions could follow on those who broke God's commandments. This would have been the default assumption for the condition of every invalid gathered around the Bethesda pool.

Jesus came to make a new covenant with the people of God. He did so by taking all those curses for disobedience to God on himself. God can still discipline his people, but it's never punitive or retributive. It's redirective and reformative, if needed, even a kind of retraining.[16] Physical afflictions are possible instruments of God's discipline.[17] But Christ's perfect obedience freed us from the curse of the broken law. As Paul Harvey once put it, life has a way of overcharging us for foolish decisions. This is true. But God is not life. There is no fear of his overcharging us once he's paid for us in full.

Jesus' warning to the man may have been retrospective, as if to say: *Have you learned nothing about the wages of sin in nearly four decades?* But his warning was also certainly looking ahead.

16. Tim Keller writes about this helpfully in *Walking with God Through Pain and Suffering*: the word "training," found in the most famous discipline passage in the New Testament, Hebrews 12:11, is the word from which *gymnasium* comes. The gymnasium, for the ancients, was a place of physical exertion as well as exposure. The word *gymnasium* translates literally as "stripped naked." Why use this word in a context of God's discipline? "When troubles and difficulties hit, we are suddenly in 'God's gymnasium'—we are exposed. Our inner anxieties, our hair-trigger temper, our unrealistic regard of our own talents, our tendency to lie and shade the truth, our lack of self-discipline—all of these things come out. Perhaps the trouble was brought on by the presence of these negative qualities . . . A good coach puts you through exercises, and what are they? They are ways to cause stress or put pressure on various parts of your body . . . A good coach will not put too much pressure on your body . . . What you need is exactly the right amount of pressure and just the right amount of discomfort and pain" (193–94).

17. 1 Cor 11:29–31; Jas 5:13–20.

Given the man's actions—that he turned Jesus into the authorities in an act of self-protection—Jesus warning him to "sin no more" seems directed at everything coming out of ongoing unbelief. A word from Jesus made him physically well. But for wholeness to take hold fully, one has to walk in repentance. The man preferred not to, it seems.

Joni Eareckson Tada, who as of this writing has lived as a paraplegic for fifty years, says the first thing she plans to do on resurrected legs is drop to grateful, glorified knees in worship of her Savior. That's what a believer wants to do. He or she is "an alleluia from head to foot," as Augustine put it.[18]

That is not the man in John 5. He doesn't worship the one who graciously healed him. We'll see worship in John 9 from one healed there. There were times when Jesus sent people he healed to priests in obedience to the law of Moses, in order for them to be cleared to return to temple worship.[19] This man went to the priests on his own to protect himself against penalties for Sabbath-breaking. Let Jesus face those consequences himself.

## Disabled in Spirit

Wasn't the man grateful for his healing? I'd like to think so. I've known some hardened people through the years. I don't think I've ever known a true ingrate, someone incapable at all of thankfulness. But the tone and tenor of this story says that something in the man's heart was chronically off.

He was disabled in spirit. It's as if Jesus says to him, *It's always been "you first" and it still is.* And what did he do with that reproof? He stayed in a "me first" mindset. He kept looking out for number one. He *ran* (!) to tell the priests Jesus broke the Sabbath, and in context this seems less an act of obedience to the law and more of a snub. It's an act of thanks-but-no-thanks to following Jesus.

Jesus applied his truth to the man as he did because he wanted the man to see himself in actual opposition to him. That seems

18. Quoted in Guinness, *Call*, 200.

19. Mark 1:40–45; Luke 5:14; 17:14.

to be the thrust of the warning about something worse happening. For a Christian to read this story and turn paranoid, looking behind our shoulder afraid that God is going to "get" us for any misstep, is to misdirect its application.

Jesus wanted the man to see that he was still disabled by unbelief. The miracle had softened his spine, but not his soul. The man was healed, but not making headway toward life in Jesus' name. He wanted to be on the good side of those who considered Jesus the epitome of a false prophet.

I'm not trying to be too hard on the man. As Frederick Buechner once quipped, we in the church are just like our biblical forebears, only more so. I too can lay around in my apathies. My appetites run amok. My strategies for dealing with sin can be moralistically self-defensive today, haphazardly self-destructive tomorrow.

I'm not smarter than those whose sins make headlines. Most of the fences I build to keep temptation out are, if I'm honest, chain link, which makes an insufficient perimeter for an enemy who burrows, scales, and shape-shifts, because sin desires to have us.[20] We love and hate our sin like Gollum loved and hated his precious ring. Our sin always strokes our ego in some way, and as G. K. Chesterton once wrote, "One may understand the cosmos but never the ego; the self is more distant than any star."[21]

By the way, Chesterton's insight is why it is treacherous to try and strike some balance between grace and truth, based on Jesus' example. We don't know ourselves as well as we think. Andy Stanley's caution is apt: "When we attempt to balance grace and truth, we get the worst of both, never the best of either. Jesus was not the balance of grace and truth. Jesus represented a full dose of both. He was full on grace and full on truth. He never dumbed down truth and he never turned down grace. He called sin 'sin' and sinners 'sinners,' and then he laid down his life to pay for their sin."[22]

20. Gen 4:7.

21. Chesterton, *Orthodoxy*, 59.

22. Stanley, *Irresistible*, 229.

## Un-Dragoned

Life in Jesus' name, as we experience it now, is marked by sensitivity to sin. That sensitivity is not morbid introspection or self-flagellation. Those are self-sanctifying tactics—trying so hard to be good for God and be an example for others that we effectively exclude the possibility of offering anyone a redeemer.[23]

Sensitivity to sin takes sin seriously, but we Christians have to preach the gospel to ourselves daily. Whatever chord "sin no more" strikes in us, it tells us at the very least that we're frequently out of tune with Jesus. My best days are really never so far removed from my worst. Jesus' work is to break our bondage to sin—to paralyze its rule over us. Sin's work is to keep us trained on ourselves, first and foremost.

I wonder if C. S. Lewis had the John 5 miracle in mind when he imaginatively spun the conversion story of a boy named Eustace, a character in *The Voyage of the Dawn Treader*. Eustace was totally self-beholding. On an island, he found a dragon's lair with treasure in it. In Lewis's allegorizing, the dragon's treasure is a stand-in for sin.

Every detail Lewis gives shows the reader how outmatched we are by our sin. Eustace casually slipped a bejeweled bracelet onto his left arm. It was too big for him at first. Aren't aspirations for life on our own in sin outsized also? Eustace then napped on a pile of coins. Doesn't laziness make us hoard our time and resources for ourselves?

Eustace awoke to discover that he'd become a dragon himself. There was nothing he could do about it. For the first time in his life, he would see how others experienced him, which was beastly.

> [Then] I [Eustace] looked up and saw the very last thing I expected: a huge lion coming slowly toward me. And one queer thing was that there was no moon last night, but there was moonlight where the lion was. So it came nearer and nearer. I was terribly afraid of it. You may think that, being a dragon, I could have knocked any lion out easily enough. But it wasn't that kind of fear. I

23. Childs, "Apologetic," 19.

> wasn't afraid of it eating me. I was just afraid of *it* . . . I knew I would have to do what it told me, so I got up and followed it.

The lion led Eustace to a garden spot. There was Bethesda-like well in the middle of it.

> I knew it was a well because you could see the water bubbling up from the bottom of it: but it was a lot bigger than most wells—like a very big, round bath with marble steps going down into it. The water was as clear as anything and I thought if I could get in there and bathe it would ease the pain [of the constricting bracelet]. But the lion told me I must undress first . . . I was just going to say I couldn't undress because I hadn't any clothes on when I suddenly thought that dragons are snaky sort of things and snakes can cast off their skins . . .

Eustace scraped at his dragon skin, trying to peel it off himself, but each time he discovered layers of dragon skin underneath. Each time he tried to enter the water his scales reappeared.

> Then the lion said . . . "You will have to let me undress you." I was afraid of his claws, I can tell you, but was pretty near desperate now. So I just lay flat down on my back and let him do it. The very first tear he made was so deep that I thought it had gone right into my heart. And when he began pulling the skin off, it hurt worse than anything I've ever felt. The only thing that made me able to bear it was just the pleasure of feeling the stuff peel off . . . I thought I'd done it myself the other three times, only they hadn't hurt . . . Then he caught hold of me—I didn't like that much for I was very tender underneath now that I'd no skin on—and threw me into the water. It smarted like anything but only for a moment. After that it became perfectly delicious and as soon I started swimming and splashing . . . I'd turned into a boy again.[24]

Eustace was "un-dragoned" by Aslan, the Christ-figure in the Narnia stories. Without the Lord's intervention, the sin we like—our greed, lusts, picking others apart—is the skin we stay in. Jesus came

24. Lewis, *Voyage*, 106–10.

to show us how scaly our sin is. It's easier to feel the scales when our sin leads to regrets and we're sorry. It's much harder when sin leads us to success—when the idea that we can go for whatever we want whenever we want it appears to be working for us.

If the healed man in John 5 heeded Jesus' direction to sin no more, he would have found, as we all do sooner or later, that he could not accomplish this on his own. Like Eustace, our efforts at self-improvement don't delve deep enough. The ethical vision of the gospel is about transcending self-interest. As Narcissus in Greek mythology wouldn't leave his pool so long as he stayed there self-beholding, we are all Narcissus in some way or another in our sin.

Where we need to start is to notice the other face behind our reflection. The Lord asks if we want to be well. The glory of God is in the face of Jesus. Rise and walk.

When the world-class Spanish cellist, Pablo Casals, was asked at the age of ninety why he still practiced the cello four to five hours a day, he replied, "Because I have the impression I am making progress."[25] If we hear the call to sin no more, we make progress by staying at our walk, running to Jesus, not away from him. Growth and progress in following Jesus is not all at once, but over a lifetime.

This is why Jesus raises us up by grace and truth to begin with. This side of heaven we'll never arrive. But we're on our feet.

25. Lindvall, *God Mocks*, 179.

# John 6:1–15

After this Jesus went away to the other side of the Sea of
Galilee, which is the Sea of Tiberias. 2 And a large crowd
was following him, because they saw the signs that he
was doing on the sick. 3 Jesus went up on the mountain,
and there he sat down with his disciples. 4 Now the
Passover, the feast of the Jews, was at hand. 5 Lifting up
his eyes, then, and seeing that a large crowd was coming
toward him, Jesus said to Philip, "Where are we to buy
bread, so that these people may eat?" 6 He said this to
test him, for he himself knew what he would do. 7 Philip
answered him, "Two hundred denarii[a] worth of bread
would not be enough for each of them to get a little." 8
One of his disciples, Andrew, Simon Peter's brother, said
to him, 9 "There is a boy here who has five barley loaves
and two fish, but what are they for so many?" 10 Jesus
said, "Have the people sit down." Now there was much
grass in the place. So the men sat down, about five thousand in number. 11 Jesus then took the loaves, and when
he had given thanks, he distributed them to those who
were seated. So also the fish, as much as they wanted. 12
And when they had eaten their fill, he told his disciples,
"Gather up the leftover fragments, that nothing may be
lost." 13 So they gathered them up and filled twelve bas-
kets with fragments from the five barley loaves left by
those who had eaten. 14 When the people saw the sign
that he had done, they said, "This is indeed the Prophet
who is to come into the world!"

15 Perceiving then that they were about to come
and take him by force to make him king, Jesus withdrew
again to the mountain by himself.

# John 6:22–71

22 On the next day the crowd that remained on the
other side of the sea saw that there had been only one
boat there, and that Jesus had not entered the boat with
his disciples, but that his disciples had gone away alone.

23 Other boats from Tiberias came near the place where
they had eaten the bread after the Lord had given thanks.
24 So when the crowd saw that Jesus was not there, nor
his disciples, they themselves got into the boats and went
to Capernaum, seeking Jesus.

25 When they found him on the other side of the
sea, they said to him, "Rabbi, when did you come here?"
26 Jesus answered them, "Truly, truly, I say to you, you
are seeking me, not because you saw signs, but because
you ate your fill of the loaves. 27 Do not work for the food
that perishes, but for the food that endures to eternal life,
which the Son of Man will give to you. For on him God
the Father has set his seal." 28 Then they said to him,
"What must we do, to be doing the works of God?" 29
Jesus answered them, "This is the work of God, that you
believe in him whom he has sent." 30 So they said to him,
"Then what sign do you do, that we may see and believe
you? What work do you perform? 31 Our fathers ate the
manna in the wilderness; as it is written, 'He gave them
bread from heaven to eat.'" 32 Jesus then said to them,
"Truly, truly, I say to you, it was not Moses who gave you
the bread from heaven, but my Father gives you the true
bread from heaven. 33 For the bread of God is he who
comes down from heaven and gives life to the world." 34
They said to him, "Sir, give us this bread always."

35 Jesus said to them, "I am the bread of life; whoever comes to me shall not hunger, and whoever believes
in me shall never thirst. 36 But I said to you that you
have seen me and yet do not believe. 37 All that the Father gives me will come to me, and whoever comes to
me I will never cast out. 38 For I have come down from
heaven, not to do my own will but the will of him who
sent me. 39 And this is the will of him who sent me, that
I should lose nothing of all that he has given me, but raise
it up on the last day. 40 For this is the will of my Father,
that everyone who looks on the Son and believes in him
should have eternal life, and I will raise him up on the
last day."

41 So the Jews grumbled about him, because he said,
"I am the bread that came down from heaven." 42 They
said, "Is not this Jesus, the son of Joseph, whose father

and mother we know? How does he now say, 'I have
come down from heaven'?" 43 Jesus answered them, "Do
not grumble among yourselves. 44 No one can come to
me unless the Father who sent me draws him. And I will
raise him up on the last day. 45 It is written in the Prophets, 'And they will all be taught by God.' Everyone who
has heard and learned from the Father comes to me—
46 not that anyone has seen the Father except he who is
from God; he has seen the Father. 47 Truly, truly, I say to
you, whoever believes has eternal life. 48 I am the bread
of life. 49 Your fathers ate the manna in the wilderness,
and they died. 50 This is the bread that comes down from
heaven, so that one may eat of it and not die. 51 I am the
living bread that came down from heaven. If anyone eats
of this bread, he will live forever. And the bread that I will
give for the life of the world is my flesh."

52 The Jews then disputed among themselves, saying, "How can this man give us his flesh to eat?" 53 So
Jesus said to them, "Truly, truly, I say to you, unless you
eat the flesh of the Son of Man and drink his blood, you
have no life in you. 54 Whoever feeds on my flesh and
drinks my blood has eternal life, and I will raise him
up on the last day. 55 For my flesh is true food, and my
blood is true drink. 56 Whoever feeds on my flesh and
drinks my blood abides in me, and I in him. 57 As the
living Father sent me, and I live because of the Father, so
whoever feeds on me, he also will live because of me. 58
This is the bread that came down from heaven, not like
the bread the fathers ate, and died. Whoever feeds on this
bread will live forever." 59 Jesus said these things in the
synagogue, as he taught at Capernaum.

60 When many of his disciples heard it, they said,
"This is a hard saying; who can listen to it?" 61 But Jesus,
knowing in himself that his disciples were grumbling
about this, said to them, "Do you take offense at this? 62
Then what if you were to see the Son of Man ascending
to where he was before? 63 It is the Spirit who gives life;
the flesh is no help at all. The words that I have spoken
to you are spirit and life. 64 But there are some of you
who do not believe." (For Jesus knew from the beginning
who those were who did not believe, and who it was who

would betray him.) 65 And he said, "This is why I told
you that no one can come to me unless it is granted him
by the Father."

66 After this many of his disciples turned back
and no longer walked with him. 67 So Jesus said to the
twelve, "Do you want to go away as well?" 68 Simon Peter
answered him, "Lord, to whom shall we go? You have the
words of eternal life, 69 and we have believed, and have
come to know, that you are the Holy One of God." 70
Jesus answered them, "Did I not choose you, the twelve?
And yet one of you is a devil." 71 He spoke of Judas the
son of Simon Iscariot, for he, one of the twelve, was going
to betray him.

# 4

# Takeout

In the eyes of the hungry there is a growing wrath.

—John Steinbeck[1]

*Eats, Shoots, and Leaves* by Lynne Truss includes an anecdote about humorist James Thurber, a writer for the *New Yorker* in the 1930s and 1940s. Thurber and his editor Harold Ross frequently clashed over comma frequency. Asked by a correspondent why Thurber put a comma in the sentence "*After dinner, the men went into the living room,*" he explained, "This particular comma was Ross's way of giving the men time to push back their chairs and stand up."[2]

Whether your chosen English translation puts a comma "after this" in the leadoff sentence of John 6 or not, we pause here to consider the pushback Jesus got in every region of his country. Buzz about Jesus did not translate to belief in him. His miracles occasioned more than a little opposition.

1. Steinbeck, *Grapes of Wrath*, 349.

2. Truss, *Eats*, 70.

Miracles in and of themselves are not watertight guides to spiritual authority or legitimacy. Counterfeit money is a thing, so too counterfeit miracles. In Deuteronomy 13, the people of God were told to be wary of the miracle-worker—to always consider the message that accompanied the miraculous. In the New Testament also, we're told to "test the spirits" (1 John 4:1).[3]

We have an appetite to be wowed, like Sergius Paulus in Acts 13, called an intelligent man yet susceptible to the spellbinding of Bar-Jesus, a false prophet Paul rebuked for blocking the way to Christ. Pharaoh's court magicians famously worked wonders, and it wasn't mere sleight of hand. There are "cosmic powers over this present darkness" (Eph 6:12) working deception.

Believers in Jesus test the spirits for alignment to Jesus' way, truth, and life. We do this not just in the presence of miracles, but in their absence also. I'm thinking here of Mohammed and Buddha. The founder of Islam refused to perform miracles to confirm he was a prophet of God. And Buddha said, "By this you shall know that a man is *not* my follower—that he tries to work a miracle."[4]

Both religions get Jesus wrong. "Every spirit that does not confess Jesus is not from God. This is the spirit of the antichrist, which you heard was coming and now is in the world already" (1 John 4:3). Whatever else one says about the spirit of antichrist, pride is baked into it. Satan in absolute haughtiness tried to get Jesus to turn craggy fields of stone into amber waves of grain. He wanted Jesus to give into appetite. It's why Jesus answered him as he did, quoting Deuteronomy: "Man shall not live by bread alone, but by every word that comes from the mouth of God" (Matt 4:4).

The people Jesus fed on the Galilean hillside knew those words from Deuteronomy. They knew the warnings in Deuteronomy about false prophets. But at that point in Jesus' ministry, they were considering him "the Prophet who is to come into the world":

> The Lord your God will raise up for you another prophet like me [Moses] from among you, from your brothers—it is to him you shall listen—just as you desired of the Lord

3. See also 2 Thess 2:9; Matt 7:21–23.
4. McDowell and Morrow, *Is God*, 23.

> your God at Horeb on the day of the assembly, when you said, "Let me not hear again the voice of the Lord my God or see this great fire anymore, lest I die." And the Lord said to me, "They are right in what they have spoken. And I will raise up for them a prophet like you from among their brothers. And I will put my words in his mouth, and he shall speak to them all that I command him. And whoever will not listen to my words that he shall speak in my name, I myself will require it of him." (Deut 18:15–19)

## The Hungry Crowd and the Full Crowd

The people on the hillside in John 6 considered Jesus a new Moses, feeding the people of God in another remote location. Later in the chapter, the people in the synagogue in Capernaum even brought up the manna of old: "What sign do you do, that we may see and believe you? What work do you perform? Our fathers ate the manna in the wilderness, as it is written, 'He gave them bread from Heaven to eat'" (John 6:30–31).

They brought this up because John says Passover was at hand (v. 4). Everyone was thinking about deliverance during Passover time. As in Egypt of old, God's people were again under the thumb of another superpower. But their memory of the manna generation was revisionist. God judged that generation for resisting his deliverer.

Notice in John 6 we have two groups of people. Let's call one the hungry crowd and the other the full crowd. John doesn't make clear where the transition to the synagogue in Capernaum took place (see v. 59). Verse 27 is as good a guess as any.[5] To that point, Jesus interacted with people from among the five thousand he fed (the hungry crowd). From that point, his interactions turned to people inside the synagogue in Capernaum (the full crowd). Those people would turn away from him when he directed them to feed on him.

5. Carson, *Gospel*, 283.

Believing the gospel Jesus personifies means accepting the provision of his grace. Jesus graciously fed the hungry crowd, but he knew he was at the same time providing for many among them who did not and would not believe in him. It was also grace to keep engaging the full crowd in the synagogue, knowing many of them would walk away from him.

In her story *The Violent Bear It Away*, Flannery O'Connor has a character, Tarwater, who tries to suppress his belief in Jesus: "In the darkest, most private part of his soul, hanging upside down like a sleeping bat, was the certain undeniable knowledge that he was not hungry for the bread of life. Had the bush flamed for Moses, the sun stood still for Joshua, the lions turned aside before Daniel only to prophesy the bread of life? Jesus? He felt a terrible disappointment in that conclusion, a dread that it was true."[6]

O'Connor read John 6 well. There is terrible disappointment in this narrative—the people being terribly disappointed with Jesus. The way he spoke about himself didn't fit with what they expected and wanted.

The hungry crowd burned a lot of calories following Jesus from place to place, "because they saw the signs that he was doing on the sick" (v. 2). That means they were hopeful. Hearts were filling up on what it would mean for Jesus to be the one they'd been hoping for. Stomachs inevitably pang, though. A boy's lunch of fish sandwiches ended up feeding everyone. It's been suggested that the bread and fish pieces must have been actually multiplying in the disciples' hands as they made distribution. That is a remarkable thing to imagine.

John specifies it was five *barley* loaves Jesus blessed. That was a poor man's loaf, each about the size of a hamburger bun. Cheap bread that hardly filled one stomach. Small fish. Nothing exotic. A five-star miracle in execution, but not gourmet. Nor was it an adventure in portion control. There were enough leftovers to fill the bed of a pickup.

6. O'Connor, *Violent*, 136.

It was a plentiful spread because grace always abounds. Where sin abounds, grace abounds all the more.[7] Where hunger abounded on a Galilean hillside, grace catered a sack lunch for thousands of people. Everything was more than it ever was before wherever Jesus went.

The hungry crowd wanted *more*. Who wouldn't? They witnessed something truly marvelous. "There is no single event in the narratives of the New Testament that so completely welded the people's attention."[8] But it wasn't more of Jesus they really wanted.

On the next day, looking for Jesus on the other side of the sea, he told them, "Truly, truly, I say to you, you are seeking me, not because you saw signs, but because you ate your fill of the loaves" (v. 26). They didn't make the connection between the sign and the meaning, the miracle and the message. As Frederick Buechner once put it in his book *Telling the Truth*, "He galvanized thousands with his miracles—healing and casting out demons and feeding a whole ballpark with his five loaves and two fish . . . the miracles didn't stick to their ribs so that he might as well have saved his strength for all the lasting good they did."[9]

It wasn't that they couldn't get the import of the miracles, as if they were slow. It was that they were unbelieving. Jesus came to fill a deeper hunger that people then and now will not receive from him.

## Filled but Empty

Jesus told the people they were focused on "the food that perishes" (v. 27). They were preoccupied with their immediate needs. And most in that culture did live hand to mouth. Daily work usually only met daily needs. Philip's calculus was it would take two hundred days of working (two hundred denarii, v. 7) to feed a crowd like Jesus did. A denarius was a day's wage for a day's food. For

7. Rom 5:20.

8. Palmer, *Intimate Gospel*, 69.

9. Buechner, *Telling the Truth*, 59.

most first-century Galileans, there were never leftovers on the tables.

By contrast, we have pantries and refrigerators and food channels on TV. I once heard someone say that our garbage disposals eat better than a large percentage of the world population. In the West, we live amid "culinary pornography," as Mark Buchanan called it: "Our preoccupation with food has entered the realm of the absurd. For example, look at any magazine—page after page of succulent, sauce-laden, sparkling, glistening food . . . We eat not out of a need for the food itself, but out of a desire for *eating* itself."[10] Buchanan goes on to call appetites run-amok idolatry.

C. S. Lewis, writing in reference to the appetite for sex, made the following parallel: "Now suppose you came to a country where you could fill a theatre by simply bringing a covered plate onto the stage and then slowly lifting the cover so as to let everyone see . . . that it contained a mutton chop or a bit of bacon, would you not think in that country something had gone wrong in the appetite for food?"[11]

A visit my family made to a Texas steakhouse during vacation one year was much like Lewis describes. A 72-ounce steak is free if you can consume it whole within an hour—along with a shrimp cocktail, salad, baked potato, and buttered roll. If not, the steakhouse keeps the $72 you put down for the attempt.

The table set aside for contestants is elevated for the rest of the diners to watch. The night we were there, two men from Missouri took the challenge. They didn't come close to making it. As the hour drained, so did the color from their faces. Every year some meet the challenge, but most just eat themselves sick.

Idolatry makes us sick through overindulgence and loves disordered. We can turn anything into an idol, including our daily bread. But even our legitimate appetites don't exist for themselves.

That is what Jesus was getting at when he told the people that for them it was about the eating, not the believing. They were full but empty. Mark Twain observed that history doesn't repeat so

10. Buchanan, *Your God*, 192.

11. Lewis, *Mere Christianity*, 91.

much as it rhymes. The hillside crowd Jesus fed rhymed with the manna generation God fed in the exodus from Egypt.

> The Israelites of old probably thought the manna and the water were simply about sustaining them through their trek through the desert. That's party true. The more spiritually aware among them probably recognized that God was teaching them something about his character, about life in his reign. And that's even more accurate. But in the fullness of time the mystery of Christ unveiled what was really at the core of God's feeding his people . . . God provided his people with bread from the sky and with water from the rock for the purpose of whetting an appetite for the gospel . . . God did not design the gospel after eating. He designed eating after the pattern of Christ, for whom and through whom all things were created (Col 1:16; John 1:1; Heb 1:2).[12]

Because they considered Jesus to be a new Moses, these descendants of the manna generation sought provisions from Jesus in service to *their* cause: another exodus. Only this time, it would be the oppressor leaving the oppressed. The Jews wanted a Messiah who would kick the Romans out of Zion. The hungry crowd was ready to beat their plowshares into swords for Jesus. The hope in their hearts was a fire in their bellies, and it didn't take much to stoke it. They were hungry to take Jerusalem back, and if Jesus were indeed the prophetic sovereign they hoped he was, he would show them in the way they wanted to be shown.

It's said that the way to a man's heart is through his stomach. That's not a gospel truth, however, as this sign event reveals. Jesus could miraculously fill stomachs just as he'd restored limbs to functionality and healed diseases. But filling the stomach with bread did not fill the heart with belief. Appreciation for a miraculous doing did not translate into allegiance. While Jesus preferred faith based on signs to no faith at all,[13] many of those who tasted the miracle in John 6 would end up alienated from Jesus.

12. Moore, *Tempted and Tried*, 73–74.

13. See John 10:38; 14:11.

## History Rhymes

Jesus made his way from the hungry crowd to a full one in a synagogue in Capernaum (v. 59). Teaching in synagogues was dialectical. It is likely that Jesus' words in John 6:27 were both parting words to the crowd on the hillside as well as introductory words for his discussion topic in the synagogue. The topic was the need to feed on him rather than being fed by him.

> "Do not labor for the food that perishes, but for the food that endures to eternal life, which the Son of Man will give to you. For on him God the Father has set his seal." Then they said to him, "What must we do, to be doing the works of God?" Jesus answered them, "This is the work of God, that you believe in him whom he has sent." So they said to him, "What sign do you do, that we may see and believe you? What work do you perform? Our fathers ate the manna in the wilderness, as it is written, 'He gave them bread from heaven to eat.'" (6:27–31)

Jesus answered that *he* was that bread from heaven. As the discussion continued, he confronted their selective memory: "Your fathers ate the manna in the wilderness, and they died" (v. 49).

History rhymes. Jesus called himself the bread of life (vv. 35, 48). He told the full crowd that he could do the types of things that he did because he came from Heaven. They replied that he was just as local as they were. Capernaum was a de facto hometown for Jesus. But the real kicker—words sure to get you kicked out of a synagogue—was when he told them his flesh was actual food and his blood real drink (vv. 51–58). They found that hard to swallow. "The Jews grumbled about him because he said, 'I am the bread that came down from heaven'" (v. 41).

Echoes of the manna generation.[14] The full crowd missed the point of the imagery, just as the hungry crowd missed the point of the miracle. And the imagery *is* difficult. It's not like that old *Seinfeld* episode in which the characters argue over whether soup

14. See Exod 16–17.

is a meal. Being fed by Jesus is one thing, but *feeding on* him? That is kind of repugnant, even when taken figuratively.

But Jesus' feed-on-me imagery was, like his miracles, aimed at a certain kind of deafness and blindness. It was aimed at people not nearly as receptive to God as they think they are.

I read a news story about a student from China attending an American university. She gave a graduation speech in which she drew a parallel between air pollution in China and the Chinese government's restrictions on free speech. Back home, she often wore a surgical mask, but then she arrived in the United States: "The moment I inhaled and exhaled outside the airport, I felt free. I would soon feel another kind of fresh air for which I will be forever grateful: the fresh air of free speech. Democracy and free speech should not be taken for granted. Democracy and freedom are the fresh air that is worth fighting for."[15]

Her home city in China took offense. Through their media outlets, they said there was nothing wrong with their air, that it was "sweet and fresh."[16] That kind of pride can't hear the truth, even when the truth is self-evident.

To feed on Jesus as the bread of life was to embrace him as God in person. Pride wouldn't allow that for Jesus' listeners in the Capernaum synagogue. They thought they knew better than him what works God required. While the hallmark of pride is a person who cannot face the truth about him or herself in relation to God, pride doesn't have to be conceited or preening. It just has to be determined to deflect the import of the truth about the person of God and ourselves in relation to him.

The full crowd in Capernaum was made up of what I'll call believing unbelievers. The desert generation Moses led, those twenty and older coming out of Egypt, died in the wilderness without going into the land. That was judgment on their unbelief.[17] Their descendants wanted to invoke the manna provision, as if all they knew was God's blessing. The full crowd in Capernaum

15. "Chinese Student Sorry," paras. 6–7.

16. "Chinese Student Sorry," paras. 11.

17. Num 32:11

brought up the manna selectively, as a point of pride, ignoring the judgment in the full telling of the story. *Our forefathers ate what Psalm 78 refers to as "the grain of Heaven, the bread of angels."*[18] *Yes,* Jesus countered, *that may be, but they still experienced judgment.*

When something offends us, even authoritative revelation from God, it is usually because it chafes our pride. In fact, our pride keeps us from realizing that we should expect authoritative revelation from God to offend us at points. Tim Keller says that if you "choose to believe only those things in the Bible that you agree with, in what way do you have a God who can contradict you?"[19]

The full crowd would not have Jesus contradict them. Jesus pressed them. He knew his imagery was offensive to them. He risked the offense to challenge their particular strain of unbelief. As Flannery O'Connor put in "The Fiction Writer and His Country," getting through sometimes requires this:

> The novelist with Christian concerns will find in modern life distortions which are repugnant to him, and his problem will be to make these appear as distortions to an audience which is used to seeing them as natural; and he may well be forced to take ever more violent means to get his vision across to this hostile audience. When you can assume that your audience holds the same beliefs you do, you can relax a little and use more normal ways of talking to it; when you have to assume that it does not, then you have to make your vision apparent by shock—to the hard of hearing you shout, and for the almost blind you draw large and startling figures.[20]

We don't put "bread of life" into the category of "large and startling figures" because we're used to the imagery. But to the original hearers in the Capernaum synagogue, Jesus' imagery was that and more. It was a heaping helping of what they didn't want on their plate. Be it nationalistic or individualistic, pride has a ravenous appetite for justifying one's unbelief.

18. Ps 78:24–25.
19. Keller, *Preaching*, 113.
20. Wood, *Flannery O'Connor*, 219.

I was once asked to be the Christian representative on a moderated panel discussion convened by an organization called American Atheists. Fundamentalism of any stripe is almost impossible to reason with, and what makes dialogue with members of the American Atheists organization hard is their belief that religion is always wrong and wrong for the world. They believe any bad things atheists do is because an individual has made wrong choices, but theists do bad because theism is inherently judgmental and hypocritical.

As a panelist, I conducted myself as graciously as I could. When barbed by the American Atheists president, who was keen to declare himself just as moral as any theist (and likely more so), I tried to stay on point and make nothing personal. The president was determined to communicate that he was a good person without God.

I knew going "large and startling" on him would only invite more defensive scorn. For the most part, the room was hoping to see the Christian mauled by their lion. When I spoke to justify my belief in and appreciation for the grace of God, I appealed to "the grace effect": how God's grace demonstrably gentles people the more genuine Christian influence holds sway, and that God's love restrains the darker impulses of human nature, and that we need something outside of ourselves to govern us.[21] I was looking for a way through their pride. But my host and his gathering already considered themselves morally superior to Christians. My appeals fell on rocky soil, for the most part.

What made the room tough was the resolve to deflect and reject any import of the truth about the person of God and us in relation to him. I used to believe that if Christians were just more winsome, more people would be drawn to our gospel. Let us be as winsome as possible, but winsomeness isn't automatically appreciated. Unbelief doesn't stand down just because you're nice.

Tish Harrison Warren wrote about how she once believed being an intelligent, winsome kind of Christian would advance the gospel smoothly. But then the university on which her campus

21. Taunton, *Grace Effect*, 22, 214–15.

organization operated turned on them for holding to an evangelical code of conduct. She says the experience revealed a subtler pride in herself: "[While] we grieve rejection, we should not be shocked or ashamed by it. That probationary year unearthed a hidden assumption that I could be nuanced or articulate or culturally engaged or compassionate enough to make the gospel more acceptable to my neighbors. But that belief is prideful. From its earliest days, the gospel has been both a comfort and an offense."[22]

Whatever is prideful in us is that which deflects or obscures, resists or rejects the truth about the person of God and ourselves in relation to him. Gospel doctrine is attractive and offensive both. Unbelief, especially when curdled by contempt, can be diamond-hard and unyielding, as the prophet Zechariah vividly pictured it.[23] But even softer expressions of unbelief have dogged reasons for keeping the person of God away.

The end of the bread-of-life dialogue came when disciples began walking out of the room. None of the Twelve did, but many hometown disciples of Jesus turned aside from him. They just couldn't accept the feed-on-me imagery.

> So close were the Twelve to the Jesus that while the word *disciple* is found in the gospels around 225 times in relationship to his followers, he applies the terms to the Twelve only on two occasions (John 13:35; 15:8). He favored expressions for the Twelve that indicate heart-bonding: "my brothers" (Matthew 12:49; 28:10; John 20:17), "children" (Mark 10:24), "friends" (John 15:15; 21:5) and "my friends" (Luke 12:4). Jesus didn't form a school; he majored on developing close relationships with the Twelve and then sending them out to serve.[24]

The Twelve stood by Jesus. Judas would betray him soon enough (vv. 70–71), but the rest were believers. Peter spoke for them: "We have believed, and have come to know, that you are the Holy One of God" (v. 69).

22. Warren, "Wrong," para. 31.
23. Zech 7:12.
24. Forman et al., *Leadership Baton*, 91.

J. R. R. Tolkien coined a word that applies to Peter's confession—*eucatastrophe*. He explained it in one of his letters:

> The sudden happy turn in a story which pierces you with a joy that brings tears (which I argued is the highest function of fairy-stories to produce). And I was there led to the view that it produces its peculiar effect because it is a sudden glimpse of Truth, your whole nature chained in material cause and effect, the chain of death, feels a sudden relief as if a major limb out of joint had suddenly snapped back. It perceives . . . that this is indeed how things really do work in the Great World for which our nature is made. And I concluded by saying that the Resurrection was the greatest "eucatastrophe" possible in the greatest Fairy Story—and produces that essential emotion: Christian joy which produces tears because it is qualitatively so like sorrow, because it comes from those places where Joy and Sorrow are at one, reconciled, as selfishness and altruism are lost in Love.[25]

Joy and sorrow are one in John 6. Sorrow for those who walked away from Jesus. Joy for those who stayed. The reason you and I know that Jesus has "the words of eternal life" is because God overcame our unbelief when we were moving in the other direction from him in our sin. The only thing you and I contributed to our redemption is getting lost. It's emphasized throughout the narrative that God works to bring us to belief (vv. 29, 37, 44, 65). Life in his name is what Jesus' signs were in service to.

## Feast On

If you're a believer, thank God for the eucatastrophe you've experienced in grace overcoming your pride. God makes us hungry for the bread of life. In the hillside miracle in John 6, as well as the explanation of it in Capernaum the next day, we find that the gospel *is* Jesus personified. The gospel is propositional in its truth

25. Tolkien, "Eucatastrophe," para. 1.

claims. But the gospel *is also and always a person*—the person of God in Jesus, full of grace and truth.

A favorite story of mine is "Babette's Feast" by Isak Dinesen.[26] It's the story of grace abounding to an austere little church in a muddy Danish fishing town. A sect of worshipers there had renounced all worldly pleasures. They wore black and ate boiled cod and a thin gruel soup made of boiling bread in water with a little beer added.

There is a Danish concept called *hygge*, which roughly translates to coziness—a tight group of friends enjoying each other around a meal.[27] That concept was lost on the Danes in Dinesen's story. The drab little group went through familiar, joyless motions. They looked like a close faith community to outsiders, but they were actually begrudged and embittered toward one another within.

A woman named Babette, a refugee from the French civil war, was sent to work for the two spinster sisters who led the sect after their father died. Though the commendation letter sent with Babette mentioned she could cook, the sisters didn't really know *who* just entered their kitchen. They showed her how to split a cod and boil the bread in the manner of their blandness. She did as they directed.

For twelve years she worked for the sisters. They treated her well. Babette did chores, helped the congregation feed the poor in the town, and did her best to keep up with their style of worship each Sunday. Though they were wary of everyone, they all considered Babette a welcome addition.

When Babette learned she'd won a lottery back in France—ten thousand francs—her winnings happened to coincide with the hundredth anniversary of the sect's founder's birth. Babette asked if she could cook a special meal for the occasion. She set about ordering supplies. It was going to be extravagant. The Danes in the village began to see deliveries they'd never seen making their

26. My telling is based on watching the movie by the same title, and also on Philip Yancey's commentary of it in *What's So Amazing*, 19–26.

27. Sayers, *Strange Days*, 155.

way to Babette's kitchen: crates of small birds, cases of champagne, fresh vegetables in overflowing wheelbarrows, even a live tortoise. The dinner was set for ten days before Christmas.

Babette managed to scrounge up some crystal and china and evergreens. She set a beautiful table for twelve. By then, the exotic food deliveries and décor made the sect members second-guess giving their permission to cook this way for them. It all felt too indulgent. Perhaps they might be committing a sin to participate. To protect her feelings, they agreed to eat Babette's feast but resist enjoying it.

A surprise guest dropped in the night of the meal. He was a military general visiting his aunt. As the dining began, the general's eyes widened with each spoonful and forkful. He was beside himself with enjoyment. He tasted Babette's quail and was transported. He exclaimed he had tasted such fare in only one place in all of Europe: Café Anglais in Paris, a restaurant renowned for its woman chef.

Babette had been that chef. Her meal that night not only moved the general, an outsider, to on-the-spot prose of appreciation, it moved the insiders too. It was impossible for them to *not* enjoy the meal. As sect members spoke warmly to one another around the table, forgiveness was asked for and given. Two members that hadn't spoken to each other in years conversed. Fond memories long embalmed were resurrected in the candlelight.

The effect of the meal on the diners was, in Dinesen's words, "as if they had indeed had their sins washed white as wool, and in this regained innocent attire were gamboling like little lambs." Only later did the sisters learn what the feast cost Babette: her entire lottery winnings. That's what a proper dinner for twelve costs at Café Anglais, Babette said.

Grace costs nothing to the recipient, but everything to the giver. Everything.

## John 6:16–21, ESV

16 When evening came, his disciples went down to
the sea, 17 got into a boat, and started across the sea to
Capernaum. It was now dark, and Jesus had not yet come
to them. 18 The sea became rough because a strong wind
was blowing. 19 When they had rowed about three or
four miles, they saw Jesus walking on the sea and coming
near the boat, and they were frightened. 20 But he said to
them, "It is I; do not be afraid." 21 Then they were glad to
take him into the boat, and immediately the boat was at
the land to which they were going.

# 5

# Sea Change

When you are in the middle of a story, it isn't a story at all. It's confusion. It's darkness. It's a lingering ache in the gut. It's stabs to the chest. It's a feeling of being swept up in a reckless current with no boat, no life jacket, and no indication of whether you are headed for calmer waters or a deeper abyss. It is only afterward, when we tell someone else these experiences, that it becomes anything like a story at all."

—Lisa Fenn[1]

I like that place in the creation account where it says, almost like an afterthought, that the Lord made the stars also.[2] Let's take a moment to ensure that this properly awes us. The sun is 93 million miles away. The North Star is 400 hundred trillion miles away. The star Betelgeuse is 880 quadrillion miles away (880 followed by fifteen zeroes).[3] That the God who can hold distances like this would come near to us is a marvel.

> In 2003, the Hubble Telescope set itself for the longest and deepest look into the universe in the history of

1. Fenn, *Carry On*, 249.
2. Gen 1:16.
3. Arthurs, *Preaching*, 76.

> astronomy. From September 24 through January 16, 2004, it performed nearly one million seconds of exposure. Researchers counted ten thousand galaxies in the frame. Doing the math, that same density across the whole area of the sky totaled two hundred billion observable galaxies (our Milky Way being just one of them). An average galaxy contains two hundred billion stars. So the total number of stars in the observable universe is a staggering forty to fifty billion trillion . . . A helpful illustration is that if each star was a dime, the pile of dimes would be as tall as the Sears Tower and cover the entire North American continent.[4]

What does one do with mind-blowing figures like these? President Teddy Roosevelt knew. An avid outdoorsman who loved the night sky, he and his friend William Beebe would take in the firmament on a clear night. They would locate the lower lefthand corner of Pegasus, then one of them would recite: "That is the Spiral Galaxy of Andromeda. It is as large as our Milky Way. It is one hundred million galaxies. It is seven hundred and fifty thousand light years away. It consists of one hundred billion suns, each larger than our own sun." There was then a pause, and Roosevelt would say, "Now I think we feel small enough! Let's go to bed."[5]

Bed is something the disciples ached for in this story now before us. But they were rowing across the Sea of Galilee. It wasn't a starry night, a celestial spray under which to look up and feel small, then dreamily drift off to sleep. The spray was coming up from below as a storm churned the waters carrying their boat. They were in trouble on the sea.

## Every Breaking Wave

Of the seven sign miracles in John's Gospel, I can enter the sound and fury of this one readily. I was once aboard a boat subjected to a sea squall. Intense experiences leave their mark.

4. DeWitt, *Eyes Wide Open*, 65–66.
5. DeWitt, *Eyes Wide Open*, 36.

I was nineteen years old. The summer after my freshman year of college was spent with a ministry in Panama City Beach, Florida. I found work aboard the Captain Anderson's Dinner Boat, a small passenger ship offering cruises across St. Andrew Bay to Shell Island. The crew cleaned the ship before and after visitors. During break times, we dove off the third deck into the warm Gulf of Mexico. Dolphins swam close. There was nothing like that summer for me.

For Shell Island to live up to its name, Captain Anderson's had to replenish its supply of shells. At designated intervals, a smaller boat in the Captain Anderson fleet was loaded with boxes of seashells. Deckhands were recruited to ride out to Shell Island and throw the shells along the shoreline for day cruisers to find.

The wind picked up as we loaded that boat one morning. Dark clouds gathered like suits in a boardroom. The smell of a downpour permeated the air. Our boat driver, a damn-the-torpedoes kind of guy, decided we should go on out. We donned yellow slickers that reeked of fish.

As expected, our boat was punished for daring to venture across the bay in storm. My coworker was built like a defensive end, but personal brawn is no match for a tossing sea. He and I huddled together to one side of the inboard motor and prayed to ride it out. Our driver cursed the pitching waves as he negotiated them. Genuine fear rose in me: *Are we getting through this?*

The storm dwindled into a gentle rain almost as fast as it had bowed up on the bay. We got to Shell Island and completed our task. But that day I learned what U2 sings in one of their songs: "Every sailor knows that the sea is a friend made enemy."[6]

All summer long the sea had been friendly to us. In an instant it wasn't. Perhaps nothing is as frightening as when the sea turns on you. I think it would be more terrifying at night.

The Sea of Galilee was a friend to Jesus' disciples. As vocational fishermen, they knew well its bounties. After the bonanza of bread and fish in John 6:1–15, Jesus told his men to get in their boat and make for the other side, for Capernaum.

6. "Every Breaking Wave," *Songs of Innocence* (2014).

I've been on a boat in the Sea of Galilee. The place is more like a large lake, but the day we sailed across it began to rain on our tour group. Everyone immediately thought of this story. It was fitting to have a wet Sea of Galilee experience. The rain was light so our boat was never in jeopardy. But as thick clouds eclipsed the surrounding landscape, it wasn't hard to imagine the fear Jesus' disciples knew on those same waters centuries earlier.

John economizes details in his version of this story. Mark and Matthew fill things in a bit more. Mark notes the hardened mood of the disciples as they rowed out. The last thing they wanted was more work after a long day. They'd been on their feet running food to thousands. Now they were putting their backs into it. They wanted a break.

We'll stick to the scene as John presents it. That doesn't mean we forget the details provided by Mark and Matthew, who gave us Peter's attempt to walk out to Jesus. It's not like John had something to hide or didn't know what Matthew and Mark knew. John was in the boat himself.

Why is Jesus' walking on the Sea of Galilee one of John's featured sign events? Because the story is a microcosm of the larger difference Jesus' coming, and coming near to us, makes. Call it a sea change between God and people.

Walking on the water was an act of glorious power. But then he did make the stars also. It was an act of grace, too. Jesus going out to his men parallels his coming to save us from our peril due to our sin. The sea change between God and people is that God takes the penalty for sin on himself, powerfully and graciously.

The Lord is triumphant over everything. Not just immediate sufferings like his disciples rowing feverishly, but everything difficult back on shore, too. Jesus triumphs over ultimate perils, ultimate sufferings, through a creative power only he has. Nothing is too difficult for him.[7] The disciples got a starboard view of Jesus using his power in grace to make the sea friendly again.

According to John (cf. 1:14), the glory of Jesus means he is imminently truthful alongside gracious. This means that nothing

7. Jer 32:17.

about him is fabricated. In each one of John's miracle narratives, including this one, Jesus tells the truth about himself and does the same. Nothing about him lies. He doesn't *seem* to be walking on water but was truly doing so. "*It is I*" is the echo of *I Am*. The truth about Jesus is that he is the Creator God personified, to whom even the elements are subject. Nothing in his dominion is outside his control.

What have we to fear? I've read scientific predictions that the stars as we know them will eventually burn out, as will our sun. The predictions say this won't happen for five billion years.[8] I don't expect the Lord to delay his return that long. But while he does, it seems much in the world is flaming out around us—governments, relationships, jobs, dreams. Our fears light up when these go dark.

As we've noted, John's interest in recording miracles was to focus a bright spotlight on Jesus' glory in service to our belief. "When we hear the word *miracle*, we must not imagine fireworks and drum rolls and trumpet blasts and then, presto, a piece of heavenly magic that sends us reeling."[9] No, we are being shown something about *reality*, that reality is only properly understood in and through Jesus, who comes to us not just as Redeemer, but also Creator.

## All of Us in the Same Boat

The theologian Stanley Hauerwas has written that what Christians believe "forces an unrelenting engagement with reality."[10] The reality is that the world is thoroughly broken and heaving under the weight and strains of sin. "Creation groans," is how Paul spoke of it in Romans 8. Miracles don't step around this but through it, through the brokenness in front of us. Miracles approach the world's brokenness and groaning, and all the fears and struggles and sufferings as a result, straight on.

8. Lightman, *Searching for Stars*, 47.

9. Peterson, *As Kingfishers Catch Fire*, 24.

10. Hauerwas, *Hannah's Child*, 45.

Miracles serve to invite belief but also develop belief in Jesus as the one sent from God, full of grace (through the action of healings and his power over physical nature) and truth (through his gospel teaching and personal interactions around miracles). John gives most of his attention in chapter 6 to the personal interactions of Jesus with the unbelieving and disbelieving. The brevity John employs for this story—"immediately the boat was at the land to which they were going" (v. 21)—serves John's larger narrative interest. He wants us his readers back ashore as quickly as possible to hear more from Jesus about what it involves and what it means to believe in a redemptive creator.

Though the disciples believed in Jesus, they would not be spared the world's brokenness. They would still know fear and frustrations of all kinds, even though they were eyewitnesses in the company of the one who hung the stars and calmed roaring seas. When Jesus asked the Twelve—at the end of chapter 6, "Do you want to go away as well?" (v. 67), and Peter answered for them, "Lord, to whom shall we go? You have the words of eternal life, and we have believed, and have come to know, that you are the Holy One of God" (vv. 68-69)—what happened the night before on the sea certainly contributed to a growing surety that God personally cared for them.

The Spanish poet Antonio Machado may have believed, "Anyone who moves forward, even a little, is like Jesus walking on the water,"[11] but no, not just *anyone* walks on water. It is a reality made possible by the glory of the one doing it. And he did it *for* his disciples. The direct objects of his grace, the beneficiaries of his power, are his people.

None of us were eyewitnesses of Jesus' glory as the original disciples were. And yet we still need to *see* his glory ourselves. Kevin DeYoung puts it plainly: "The biggest need in your life, and in mine, is to see the glory of God in the face of Jesus Christ." But how do we?

11. Quoted in Lamott, *Hallelujah Anyway*, 136.

> I'm convinced that more evangelism, more prayer, more fruitfulness, more holiness will flow from the fountain of our lives only when we start drinking more deeply of Christ. If you want to be more merciful, look upon Jesus who cried out at the cross, "Father forgive them, for they know not what they do." If you want to be more loving, look upon Jesus who ate with sinners and welcomed repentant prostitutes and tax collectors into the kingdom. If you want to be purer, look upon Jesus whose eyes are like flames of fire and whose feet are like burnished bronze. If you want more courage in the face of lies and injustice, look upon Jesus who drove out the money changers from the temple with a whip. If you want to be stronger in the midst of suffering, look upon Jesus who did not revile when reviled and submitted himself wholly to the will of his Father. If you want to grow in grace, look upon Jesus who reinstated Peter after he denied his Lord three times. If you want more tenderness in your life, look upon Jesus who took the little children upon his lap and blessed them. If you want to display the diverse excellencies of God, look upon Jesus who came from the Father full of grace and truth. Our main problem is not lack of time or resources or the annoying people in our lives. Your main problem and my main problem is that we do not see enough the glory of God in the face of Jesus Christ.[12]

Jesus' walking on water adds another line to DeYoung's litany. If you want to keep from doing deep dives into fear, look upon Jesus, who said, "Do not be afraid." He did not just say it in verse 20 in our story. It was *the* imperative statement Jesus repeated most often in the Gospels. Some twenty times he is on record uttering some restatement of *do not be afraid*.

Fear is our recognition that the world is not how it is supposed to be. Jesus revealing his glory in all the ways he did makes an actual difference in reality as we experience it and engage it. The action of Jesus coming to his men in the boat saved them from their trouble in the moment. He supernaturally controlled the elements. He was present to them in their need. That's how

12. DeYoung, "What We Need Most," paras. 2–11.

grace works. They saw his glory through his grace to them and it checked their fears, immediately and eventually for the long term. Not all fear is equal, however. We need to qualify what kind of fear Jesus quiets. It is appropriate to fear walking barefoot in tall grasses next to bodies of water where I live. Snakes inhabit those grasses in the warm months, some of them poisonous.

It is appropriate to fear getting too close to the cliff edges when visiting the Grand Canyon National Park. A park ranger told us during our visit there that those who die in the park every year do because they do not fear the cliff edge enough. "It's usually middle-aged men showing off for their families," he said with a sigh. But then acrophobia—the extreme fear of heights—would cause one to miss God's splendor in that park altogether. That's an unhealthy fear.

The world is a frightening place, we know. There are wars and rumors of wars. There is nature, red in tooth and claw. Disease. Terrorism. Corruption in high places. Hundred-year storms. A friend told me about his son-in-law in Houston, Texas, surveying flood damage to his neighborhood during Hurricane Harvey in 2017. Wading through waist-deep water, he saw an alligator swim up his street. He quickly got to higher ground. That's healthy fear.

The world is a frightening place because we all live in the wake of our collective rebellion against our creator. Creation groans like the "big old ship" J. F. Powers described in his novel: "She creaks, she rocks, she rolls, and at times she makes you want to throw up."[13] Or as Kanye West conveyed in his 2004 rap hit, "Jesus Walks":

> Yo, we at war
> We at war with terrorism, racism
> But most of all, we at war with ourselves
> (Jesus walks)
> God show me the way because the Devil's trying to break me down
> (Jesus walks with me)

13. Quoted in Yancey, *Church: Why Bother?*, 17.

> The only thing I pray is that my feet don't fail me now (I want Jesus)
> (Jesus Walks)
> And I don't think there is nothing I can do now to right my wrongs
> (Jesus Walks with me)
> I want to talk to God, but I'm afraid because we ain't spoke in so long
> (I want Jesus).[14]

Read West's lines again. He's facing fears that both arrive and emerge. Fears that arrive come from outside ourselves: terrorist attacks, natural disasters, market crashes, joblessness due to corporate downsizing. In Henry James's words: "Life *is* a battle. On this point optimists and pessimists agree. Evil is insolent and strong; beauty enchanting but rare; goodness very apt to be weak; folly very apt to be defiant; wickedness to carry the day; imbeciles to be in very great places, people of sense in small, and mankind generally, unhappy."[15]

Fears that emerge come from inside ourselves—those what-if scenarios our minds play on loop. Even more existential fears lurk deeper down. What if I lose my spouse, or my child, or my job? West gives voice to one of the deepest human fears when he articulates that there may be nothing he can do to right his wrongs. He fears being denied God's forgiveness. He fears that his desire to speak with God about his life will go unwelcomed "because we ain't spoke in so long."

The gospel declares us to all be in the same boat. But its a boat Jesus walks out to, lurching and tossed about as it is, and speaks his presence: *It is I. Do not be afraid.*

"If I take the wings of the morning and dwell in the uttermost parts of the sea, even there your hand shall lead me, and your right hand shall hold me. If I say, 'Surely the darkness shall cover me, and the light about me be night,' even the darkness is not dark

14. I became aware of these lyrics from Knut M. Heim, "Lord Is My Shepherd," 56.

15. Epstein, *Narcissus Leaves the Pool*, 226.

to you; the night is bright as the day, for darkness is as light with you."[16]

## Bearing the Burden of Hoping

How Jesus comes to us is in and through his people, most often. In a dark season in our family, full of its own kinds of winds and waves, I reached out to another pastor in my city for counsel. He knew firsthand where I was as a father. The traumatic event in my life had happened to him too. I offered to meet him at his office, since I was the one initiating a meeting and we didn't know each other. But he told me he would come to me.

That simple act of coming to me ministered deeply. He gave me more than counsel. He gave me hope. I realized later I needed him to come to me. In saying he would come to me, he immediately allayed whatever fear I generated that he might take my reaching out to him as a nuisance. Jesus was there for me in that act, reminding me through it that my situation was not lost to him. *It is I. Do not be afraid.*

Jesus may not come to us and for us right away. The text says his men were three to four miles out. That takes some time when you're rowing and fighting whipping winds. If we're forced to wait, or feel we're having to exhibit patience, we can despair in our fears. *Will he ever come?*

Someone gave me a definition of patience once, that it is bearing the burden of hoping. My experience of God in storms of life has been a crazy, holy grace, as Frederick Buechner has called it. We have a grandson now, born out of the storm we were in with an unmarried child of ours. That was crazy. But our grandson was born to God's good purposes for him. That is holy.

> Once during the illness of my oldest daughter, who had anorexia almost to the point of death, a friend of mine—a very recent friend, I didn't know him awfully well—knew about this trouble in my life. He was a minister in

16. Ps 139:9–12.

> Charlotte, North Carolina, where I'd been on some sort of speaking thing. And one day in Vermont, the phone rang. I picked it up and here was my friend on the other end. And I said, "O my golly, Lou, how nice to hear from you. How are things in Charlotte?" He said, "Well, I'm not in Charlotte. I'm in Manchester." Manchester, Vermont, is perhaps fifteen minutes away from where I live. And I said, "What do you mean you're in Manchester?" And he said, "Yeah, I knew it was a bad time for you; I just thought it might be nice to have somebody, an extra friend, around." And I just thought, *My God, I might not even have been here.* Of course, if he'd called me ahead of time and said, "I'll think I'll come up to see you," I would've said, "Don't even dream of such a preposterous thing." I wouldn't have allowed it. He knew that. So instead, he came eight hundred miles in an airplane and found himself a room at a hotel, taking the chance that I would be there, which I was. And I was moved to the very soles of my feet by that experience. And so was he, of course. So was he.[17]

That's how Jesus walks out to us in our frayed nerves and flagging spirits. We don't bear the burden of hoping alone. If I know anything at this point in my career as a parent and pastor, it's that I want to be where he is, and he is among his people who practice empathy and grace.

Did it move Jesus to walk out to his men and find them struggling? I used to picture Jesus as rather workmanlike in the execution of his ministry. Not stern, but my default mode in thinking of a holy demeanor was cultivated detachment. In that vein I didn't regard Jesus as very *personable.* He was with people, of course, but I suppose I pictured him as more often than not a bit annoyed by people.

In walking out on the raging water, Jesus entered his men's suffering. I picture not a steely gaze at them straining at their oars but compassion. It was, for them, a bad day at the office. (How much of our suffering in life takes place in and around our

17. Buechner, *Crazy, Holy Grace*, 27.

vocations?) In walking out to them, he entered their suffering in order to dispel their fears that they would shipwreck and not survive. He could have made shelter for himself ashore, even placed himself in Capernaum to await their haggard arrival. Those with power have been known to preserve themselves at the expense of those under them.

But he went out to them. It was a powerful action. It was also grace.

We sometimes wonder where God is in the midst of our crises. We wonder if he's aloof and distant and thereby unconcerned or unable to help us. But the cross serves to remind us that God enters human suffering personally, in order to do something definitive about it.

At first sight, the disciples didn't recognize Jesus. They were afraid of his approach. You have to look at this from their vantage point: the ancients had no way to get down into the depths of the sea and study what was there. In the absence of scientific study, superstitions developed. It was thought the sea was a haunt for menacing spirits. Who really knew what prowled about deep under the surface? And then atop the waters comes Jesus—of course "they were frightened" (v. 19)! We would be too in those circumstances. Jesus walked on the water as if he was striding along the Jericho Road.

It's only when he speaks that they recognize who it is. But he sent them to row across the Sea of Galilee, and he knew the storm would surge against them. Why not just keep them from that to begin with?

## Harbor for Us

Believing in Jesus isn't about learning how to avoid what frightens us. It's about listening for him when we're in what frightens. That is the faith Jesus is working to develop in us. Not that we'll never know storms of life. We get no guarantee from Jesus that we'll be spared any of life's harder edges. Believing in Jesus is about learning how, within our fears, to pivot to his character; how to turn and face Jesus in and with them. We do that by listening to him—listening for him—in his word and people.

That Jesus came to us personally is the greatest truth I know. It's how I know God is not just up there but never here. We have fears of all kinds crowding into our lives. But the gospel at its core addresses one central, throbbing fear: *What if the God who is there is never here for me?* We confront this fear when we face ourselves as sinners. Perhaps the God I've wronged will leave me to my just desserts?

G. K. Chesterton said something to the effect that when a man really tells the truth, the first truth he tells is that he himself is a liar. I don't have to fear God finding this out. He knows it's true about me already. But because it's true, what if God allowed my life to capsize and me to drown in my sin and its consequences?

Some in fear will project onto God the values clarification exercise about the lifeboat adrift at sea—the one where a doctor and young mom and pro athlete and sailor and a celebrated professor and a trash collector are in a lifeboat, and one of them has to be tossed overboard for the rest to survive. Who's it going to be? Will God value me in the end, or toss me out and let me sink?

You know why the gospel is good news? Because God does not work by values clarification. If Jesus is the glory of God personified, that glory means he has unlimited creative power and is imminently truthful. His coming into the world marks an absolute sea change between God and people. If Jesus is the glory of God coming to me, this means that nothing about my sin is unknown to him, and nothing about my sin is too difficult for him to handle and overcome. Only this understanding will free us from our deepest fears.

If you've seen the movie *The Shawshank Redemption*, you'll remember the scene where the prisoner defies the warden and plays an opera song over the loudspeaker. Red Redding narrates the effect this way: "I have no idea to this day what those two Italian ladies were singing about . . . I like to think they were singing about something so beautiful it can't be expressed in words, and makes your heart ache because of it. I tell you those voices soared, higher and farther than anybody in a gray place dares to dream. It was like some beautiful bird flapped into our drab little cage and made these walls dissolve away . . . and for the briefest of moments, every last man at Shawshank felt free."

In a place of despairing, that music walked into their hearts. The gospel we believe is uniquely beautified by this walking-on-the-water story. You and I are not left in our peril fearing that we can't and won't make harbor. Jesus is going to be the harbor for us. "Jerusalem will be told: 'Don't be afraid. Dear Zion, don't despair. Your God is present among you, a strong Warrior there to save you. Happy to have you back, he'll calm you with his love and delight you with his songs'" (Zeph 3:17, Message).

This is the sea change between God and people: God comes to us in Jesus to be the harbor we need. Whatever sufferings follow or fears threatening, my life is his. The believed gospel checks all fears of being in anyway lost to God. If God applies to me the merits of Christ—if he sends Jesus out to the boat we're all in to save us—then his care for you and me is more than we can fathom.

I love an observation by Ravi Zacharias, that when we look at the instructions for the ark God had Noah build, there is no mention of a rudder. God would harbor the occupants of that ship himself. Centuries later, the same happens again on the Sea of Galilee. Men desperately needing a harbor get one in Jesus walking out to get into the boat with them. The story shows us that God is himself the harbor we need in Jesus.

The way of Jesus with us in redemption is how journalist Dennis Covington remembers his father getting him to come home when he was a boy playing down by a neighborhood lake:

> It's afternoon at the lake. The turtles are moving closer to shore. The surface of the water is undisturbed, an expanse of smooth, gray slate. Most of the children in my neighborhood are called home for supper by their mothers. They open the doors, wipe their hands on their aprons, and yell, "Willie!" or "Joe!" or "Ray!" Either that or they use a bell, bolted to the doorframe and loud enough to start the dogs barking in backyards all along the street. But I was always called home by my father, and

> he didn't do it in the customary way. He walked down the alley all the way to the lake. If I was close, I could hear his shoes on the gravel before he came into sight. If I was far, I would see him across the surface of the water, emerging out of shadows into the gray light. He would stand with his hands in his pockets of his windbreaker while he looked for me. This is how he got me to come home. He always came to the place I was before he called my name.[18]

Glory accessible. Grace and truth remarkable. *It is I*, Jesus says to you and me still. *Do not be afraid.*



18. Covington, *Salvation on Sand Mountain*, 239–40.

# John 9:1–41, ESV

As he passed by, he saw a man blind from birth. 2 And
his disciples asked him, "Rabbi, who sinned, this man or
his parents, that he was born blind?" 3 Jesus answered,
"It was not that this man sinned, or his parents, but
that the works of God might be displayed in him. 4 We
must work the works of him who sent me while it is day;
night is coming, when no one can work. 5 As long as I
am in the world, I am the light of the world." 6 Having
said these things, he spit on the ground and made mud
with the saliva. Then he anointed the man's eyes with the
mud 7 and said to him, "Go, wash in the pool of Siloam"
(which means Sent). So he went and washed and came
back seeing.

8 The neighbors and those who had seen him before
as a beggar were saying, "Is this not the man who used to
sit and beg?" 9 Some said, "It is he." Others said, "No, but
he is like him." He kept saying, "I am the man." 10 So they
said to him, "Then how were your eyes opened?" 11 He
answered, "The man called Jesus made mud and anointed my eyes and said to me, 'Go to Siloam and wash.' So I
went and washed and received my sight." 12 They said to
him, "Where is he?" He said, "I do not know."

13 They brought to the Pharisees the man who
had formerly been blind. 14 Now it was a Sabbath day
when Jesus made the mud and opened his eyes. 15 So
the Pharisees again asked him how he had received his
sight. And he said to them, "He put mud on my eyes,
and I washed, and I see." 16 Some of the Pharisees said,
"This man is not from God, for he does not keep the Sabbath." But others said, "How can a man who is a sinner
do such signs?" And there was a division among them.
17 So they said again to the blind man, "What do you say
about him, since he has opened your eyes?" He said, "He
is a prophet."

18 The Jews did not believe that he had been blind
and had received his sight, until they called the parents of
the man who had received his sight 19 and asked them,
"Is this your son, who you say was born blind? How then
does he now see?" 20 His parents answered, "We know
that this is our son and that he was born blind. 21 But

how he now sees we do not know, nor do we know who opened his eyes. Ask him; he is of age. He will speak for himself." 22 (His parents said these things because they feared the Jews, for the Jews had already agreed that if anyone should confess Jesus to be Christ, he was to be put out of the synagogue.) 23 Therefore his parents said, "He is of age; ask him."

24 So for the second time they called the man who had been blind and said to him, "Give glory to God. We know that this man is a sinner." 25 He answered, "Whether he is a sinner I do not know. One thing I do know, that though I was blind, now I see." 26 They said to him, "What did he do to you? How did he open your eyes?" 27 He answered them, "I have told you already, and you would not listen. Why do you want to hear it again? Do you also want to become his disciples?" 28 And they reviled him, saying, "You are his disciple, but we are disciples of Moses. 29 We know that God has spoken to Moses, but as for this man, we do not know where he comes from." 30 The man answered, "Why, this is an amazing thing! You do not know where he comes from, and yet he opened my eyes. 31 We know that God does not listen to sinners, but if anyone is a worshiper of God and does his will, God listens to him. 32 Never since the world began has it been heard that anyone opened the eyes of a man born blind. 33 If this man were not from God, he could do nothing." 34 They answered him, "You were born in utter sin, and would you teach us?" And they cast him out.

35 Jesus heard that they had cast him out, and having found him he said, "Do you believe in the Son of Man?" 36 He answered, "And who is he, sir, that I may believe in him?" 37 Jesus said to him, "You have seen him, and it is he who is speaking to you." 38 He said, "Lord, I believe," and he worshiped him. 39 Jesus said, "For judgment I came into this world, that those who do not see may see, and those who see may become blind." 40 Some of the Pharisees near him heard these things, and said to him, "Are we also blind?" 41 Jesus said to them, "If you were blind, you would have no guilt; but now that you say, 'We see,' your guilt remains.

# 6

## Now See Here

But what every man has not a right to do, is to make others believe that faith is something lowly, or that it is an easy thing, whereas it is the greatest and the hardest.

—Søren Kierkegaard[1]

Either John didn't catch the name of this "man blind from birth" or elected to leave it out of the record. If assigning him a name for something like a play adaptation, I think I'd call him "Jeff," in memory of a blind man I pastored. My Jeff had a moxie similar to this man we meet in the sixth miracle story John gave us.

Jeff was a character, as we say of our eccentrics in the South. Colorful. Off-color. His blindness was due to complications from juvenile diabetes, which compromised his health overall. He used a white stick and a black lab, a guide dog named Norma Jean, whom he fattened on all the candy he fed her. Jeff always sat on the front row in church, Norma Jean lying at his feet. He played with her leash throughout the service, twirling it like a short lasso.

1. Kierkegaard, *Fear and Trembling*, 80.

Sometimes Jeff removed his sunglasses to put a monocle eyepiece up to his "good eye" in order to just make out a shape or color. Though he liked to wisecrack, Jeff could be combative. I had to talk him out of suing the church once. He felt snubbed that someone allergic to pet dander was hosting a Christmas party. In his view it discriminated against him that Norma Jean could not be allowed inside.

I visited Jeff in the hospital during his final illness. He called a few days later, trying to speak through heavy sobs. Doctors had told him they might have to amputate parts of his feet. "My body has suffered so much," he said. "I can't take anymore of this." Already mobility-challenged, Jeff dreaded a wheelchair more than anything.

He asked me at times why God didn't heal him. He thought he must have made God mad at him somewhere along the way. I tried to talk him out of that notion too, but it was like a fishhook in his spirit.

Jeff is with the Lord now. His faith is sight. Questions no longer gnaw at him. In Jesus' day, a person's blindness triggered questions too. Questions in answer form, like how questions function on the game show *Jeopardy*. Everyone back then knew what congenital blindness was: *What is punishment by God?*

The Pharisees believed that. So did the disciples. Perhaps they were just trying to wrap their minds around *why* when they asked Jesus about the man born blind. But then they likely assumed that Jesus agreed with their cause-effect correlation that bad things happen to bad people.

The problem in believing that is twofold: First, "bad things happen to bad people" is a doctrine of karma, not grace. Bono, front man for the Irish rock group U2, famously told a journalist that the reason he's a Christian is because God is *not* karmic but gracious: "The center of all religions is the idea of Karma. You know, what you put out comes back to you . . . I'd be in big trouble if Karma was finally going to be my judge . . . It doesn't excuse my mistakes, but I'm holding out for Grace. I'm holding out that Jesus took my sins onto the cross, because I know who I am, and I hope I don't have to depend on my own religiosity."[2]

The other part of the problem when we believe suffering is direct deposit compensation for sin is that every one of us is in rebellion against God. If the disciples' logic was carried to its conclusion, all should be born blind or otherwise disabled. "This is *the judgment*," Jesus said earlier in John (3:19): "the light has come into the world, and people loved the darkness rather than the light because their works were evil." In a sentence, that describes the spiritual blindness that is our natural state. Spiritual blindness is pervasive—this is why Jesus repeated his prerogative to judge it in our story: "*For judgment* I came into this world, that those who do not see may see, and those who see may become blind" (v. 39).

Jesus asked his disciples to replace their flawed judgment with his: *What if I told you this man was born blind in order to show those who think they see that they don't?* The Pharisees would scoff at that, of course. Like Pastor Merrill in John Irving's novel *A Prayer for Owen Meany*, religion had become their brand: "He taught the same old stories, with the same old cast of characters; he preached the same old virtues and values; he theologized on the same old 'miracles'—yet he appeared not to believe in any of it."[3]

## How to Become a Pharisee

H. G. Wells wrote a short story in which a man happened upon a community of blind people. Entirely cut off from civilization, their blindness had been passed down through fourteen generations. Even the concept of sight was lost on them. As the visitor tried to explain to them what it means to see, he found it completely beyond their comprehension.[4]

Wells's story parallels the way Jesus found the Pharisees, who figure prominently in this story. Their self-imposed blindness was

2. Assayas, *Bono*, 204.
3. Irving, *Prayer for Owen Meany*, 551.
4. DeWitt, *Eyes Wide Open*, 22.

born of pride and fed by power. Christians tend to be hard on the Pharisees, and for good reason: we only know them as Jesus' enemies. They sought not just to subvert his teaching, but to kill him. If we set the Gospels to a musical score, whenever the Pharisees appear, the notes would be heavy, ominous.

And yet the nation owed its Pharisees a great debt of gratitude. They were the ultimate patriots. "Pharisee" means "the separated one." When the Greeks tried to impose pagan Hellenism by force three hundred years before Jesus' birth, the Pharisees formed as an opposition party with a noble objective: preserve the worship of the one true God at the heart of Jewish identity. Before self-righteousness took them over, Pharisees ensured that Israel remembered her covenant with God. It was the Pharisees who kept the people of God aware that, even though they were under foreign powers, they were still called to be an uncompromisingly holy nation.[5]

So what happened to the Pharisees? How was it that, "by the time Jesus showed up, they had somehow lost the vision of the kingdom of God and had become obsessively concerned with every conceivable item of dress or behavior that went into being a Jew"?[6]

My wife and I once stayed with a friend whose home has a panoramic view. One side of his living room is floor-to-ceiling windows looking out over purple mountain majesty. What if, while staying there, I began to notice spider webs on those windows? Rain streaks, also. Dirt. Dust. Smudge prints here and there.

Let's say I get cleaning supplies and go to work on the windows. My back is to the breathtaking scene behind me, my focus on the glass before me. I wake up the next day and look at the windows again. During the night crawly bugs made crisscross trails on the windows. A moth crash-landed in one spot. The spiders were busy again too. I go back outside and clean.

The next day I find frost and more spots on the window—spots I somehow missed previously! This time I dedicate the

5. Exod 19:6.

6. Peterson, *Jesus Way*, 211.

morning to cleaning the windows, canceling a planned hike with my wife. I go into town to find more potent cleaning solutions. I decide that cleaning the windows is really the most important part of our stay. I tell myself the view outside those windows is too great for the windows to be anything less than pristine.

What if that went on day after day after day? I've become a Pharisee, like we have them presented to us in the Gospels. I've been cleaning those windows so that when I look *at* them I don't see anything *on* them. But they were installed to look *through*. If I'm not looking through them at the scenery beyond them, I may as well be blind to it.

That is what happened to the Pharisees. God's law was a window for keeping in view what an awesome thing it is for an all-sufficient, infinitely holy being to take a people to love. He doesn't need any of us. But he desires us. He set the Jewish nation apart to bless the whole world through them. Somewhere along the way, however, Pharisees stopped looking through the law at God. They started looking at the law and missed God.

> Because of this slow change from an interior passion to an exterior performance and the shift of attention from the majesty of God to housecleaning for God, the Pharisees at the time of Jesus were not, as a group, very attractive. All the same, they represented the best of Judaism. They at least were in touch with their heritage; they knew they were Jews first and always; they studied their Scriptures and knew them inside and out; and they were proud heirs to this vigorous and fierce preservation of Jewish identity.[7]

This is the tension in John 9—why it was quite a thing to tell the bravehearts of Israel's society that they were effectively blind to what really mattered to God. "If you were blind, you would have no guilt; but now that you say, 'We see,' your guilt remains" (v. 41). The Pharisees saw in Jesus someone smudging up their windows, if not breaking them.

7. Peterson, *Jesus Way*, 212. My illustration of the window is inspired by a similar illustration Peterson uses in his book.

It could have been primarily for the benefit of the Pharisees that Jesus healed the man with a makeshift mud poultice. A last-ditch attempt to get through to them. What better way to communicate to housecleaners for God, men who prided themselves in their separateness, that they'd only succeeded in making themselves *too clean* for God? That's the effect of self-righteousness. Self-righteousness is like so much mud caking our eyes. It's got to be washed away.

In this narrative, the heroically religious were unbelieving. Most people thought of the Pharisees as the ones closest to God. They certainly thought of themselves that way. But that's the tragedy of the Pharisees. While they formed to valiantly oppose Israel's every threat, they ended up considering Israel's God in flesh a threat to violently oppose. They seethed at Jesus. They didn't see.

## All the Light We Cannot See

Healing congenital blindness was something no one before Jesus did. It's hard to overemphasize how miraculous a miracle it was. The Pharisees were right to investigate it because it was unprecedented. They were wrong to let their investigation mutate into an interrogation of the recipient.

To that point, no prophet had ever healed blindness. Prophets like Elijah and Elisha were given power to bring two boys back to life.[8] Elisha, furthermore, struck an invading army with temporary blindness.[9] Jewish tradition records a couple of alleged healings from blindness, but there is no record in Scripture of this kind of healing until Jesus.[10]

Rabbis considered the healing of blindness a greater feat than raising the dead. Many Pharisees would have believed that. They believed miracles were possible, unlike their Sadducee brothers from across the aisle in the Sanhedrin. The healed man himself

8. 1 Kgs 17:17–24 and 2 Kgs 4:18–37.

9. 2 Kgs 6:18.

10. Carson, *Gospel*, 374.

was appropriately blown away by what happened to him: "Never since the world began has it been heard that anyone opened the eyes of a man born blind" (v. 32). He wasn't embellishing things.

As mentioned, his blindness was not just personally difficult but relationally alienating. Most were suspicious of him: he *had to be* under God's rebuke. So strongly was that the prevailing sense of things that I suspect the man sometimes wondered if it was really true in his case. *Is everyone right about me?* Jesus said there was, in fact, a reason for the man's blindness: "that the works of God might be displayed in him" (v. 3).

God is always doing more than we know. That providence extends over anything we have to bear. But Jesus' reply to his disciples' question about the man born blind was an answer and nonanswer at the same time. It still doesn't tell us *why* the man *had to be* blind all those years. We're placed in the tension articulated in Deuteronomy 29:29, that some things are revealed to us by God and some things remain known only to God. "The secret things—God's reasons, intentions, and plans in the trillions of circumstances in the world every day—are innumerable . . . God has reasons why certain trials have entered our lives, and we only have access to an infinitesimal fraction of his reasons."[11]

In her book, *Everything Happens for a Reason (And Other Lies I've Loved)*, Kate Bowler tells about her sojourn through Stage 4 cancer. More than the cancer itself, she felt that people opinionating on why she had it, or what God was doing in it and through it, would ultimately do her in. Bowler called it "the trite cruelty in the logic of the perfectly certain," and "spray painting everything in gold." After writing about her health battle in a highly trafficked *New York Times* article, she said:

> My in-box is full of strangers giving reasons. People offer them to me like wildflowers they picked along the way. A few people want me to cultivate spiritual acceptance . . . But most everyone I meet is dying to make me certain. They want me to know, without a doubt, that there is a hidden logic to this seeming chaos. Even

11. Cole, *Therefore I Have Hope*, 109.

> when I was still in the hospital, a neighbor came to the door and told my husband that everything happens for a reason. "I'd love to hear it," he replied. "Pardon?" she said, startled. "The reason my wife is dying," he said in that sweet and sour way he has, effectively ending the conversation as the neighbor stammered something and handed him a casserole.[12]

The attempt to plumb "reasons for" a travesty or trial is awkward for us. Plenty are ready to deploy platitudes to help us fix it. Make it better. That's all well-intentioned, usually, but even when the reason is known, it can still be difficult to square with. Knowing the reason doesn't mean we will like it.

Reasons are like points of light on the electromagnetic spectrum. There is light we can and cannot see. Or like diving down into the ocean; there is a depth at which the pressure becomes too great and we have to surface. What do we surface to?

John said he narrated seven miracles so that we might believe in Jesus, and in believing have life in his name (John 20:31). The story of Jesus healing the man blind from birth with mud and a wash in the waters of Siloam is a story about belief and unbelief. Our belief in Jesus, our life in his name, is what we surface to again and again, not just when we're submerged in troubles.

The blind man believed in Jesus through what Jesus did for him. He *saw* Jesus for who he was. The Pharisees, though witnesses to great miracles, remained mired in unbelief. They refused to see. They rejected life in Jesus' name.

Belief sees. Unbelief blinds. The blind man's belief in Jesus saw its way to worship. The Pharisees' unbelief was blindness to their own self-righteousness. Unbelief can be blind to unrighteousness also, but in this story, unbelief is blind to self-righteousness.

## Belief Sees and Speaks

The blind man's belief saw its way to worship and to witness. The worship is mentioned specifically in verse 38. Most of the chapter

12. Bowler, *Everything Happens*, 112–13.

is the man's witness before the Pharisees. Proverbs 28:1 says that the righteous are as bold as a lion. Now seeing, the man's witness practically roars to the Pharisees with righteous indignation. *Now see here!*

I once asked a well-known preacher what he considered to be the greatest challenge facing the church in the twenty-first century. Without blinking, he said, "Failure of nerve in the efficacy of preaching."[13] In his observation, preachers had fallen into a mindset that we have to make the Bible relevant, and thereby resort to gimmickry and absolutizing present concerns. As Stanley Hauerwas once put it, we think our task is to make the gospel intelligible to the world, when really our task is to help the world understand why it will never be intelligible without the gospel.

In a way, that was the blind man's task before the Pharisees once Jesus gave him sight. *Can you men intelligibly speak for God when you reject his servant?* Almost no one dared stand up to the Pharisees. There was no failure of nerve in the man's witness. To reinforce this, John includes the detail of how afraid the man's parents were of the Pharisees. But their son had a different spirit. It was almost as if he'd waited his whole life to witness to the powerful of the power of God. *Now see here*, he said to those casting doubt on what he'd experienced, "one thing I do know, that though I was blind, *now I see*" (v. 25, emphasis mine).

No one would take that from him. He wasn't standing before them as a perfect man, but a man who had a life-changing experience with Jesus. He incarnated the battle cry of *Friday Night Lights*: "Clear eyes, full hearts, can't lose." The man born blind, once sighted, buckled a chinstrap and prepared to take some hits for his worship of Jesus.

I've heard Christians say we should always preach the gospel and sometimes use words. That line is attributed to Saint Francis of Assisi, but there's no evidence he said it. In fact, it would have been an odd thing to say for someone who sometimes preached five times a day.

13. Personal conversation with Stuart Briscoe in 2008.

The idea that our lives speak louder than our words—call it "osmosis witness." It's true that words can be cheap and people are dismissive of mere rhetoric. But even so, our example in believing is no substitute for speaking about our belief. The gospel of faith in Jesus, of our need for his righteousness to cover our sin, is a *spoken* message. If we minimize this, hoping our life communicates for us, we can end up preaching the gospel of what-a-nice-person-I-am, which saves no one.

We tend to assume too much about the power of our example anyway. People often get the tune of a song before they get the lyrics, but the lyrics still matter. There is a place in John Calvin's writings where he describes how certain Roman Catholic friends reacted negatively to the rules and regulations of the church. They were saying no one needed that; Christians just needed to love one another. "As if that's easier!" Calvin said.[14] The world will know those in Christ by our love—Jesus said so[15]—but they won't *know* him, the object of our love, without some spoken context.

We don't stand before Pharisees today in our witness to Jesus saving us out of spiritual blindness. But we do find around us those who are every bit as dedicated as the Pharisees of old to opposing our specific witness to Jesus as God. While Pharisees wanted to enforce belief in God their way, many around us want belief in God kept to ourselves.

The man blind from birth, once healed by Jesus, knew that Jesus was God. And that wouldn't at all make life easier for him in a Pharisee-controlled society. It got him kicked out of the synagogue, a fate more socially ostracizing than his blindness had been.

We see in this story that the way of faithful witness may cost us something. Gospel opposition takes many forms—including from those who seem to be insiders. Have you ever been the conscience for a believing friend, much like this man was trying to be to the Pharisees? But the friend wants to hold on to their sin and tells you you're being judgmental. I've been there.

14. Quoted in Horton, *Christless Christianity*, 134.

15. John 13:35.

We have to watch our tone and not convey scolding. Nobody likes that. But the blind man's *now see here* tone was appropriate to take with people who really should have seen that Jesus' work had the fingerprints of God all over it. "If this man were not from God, he could do nothing" (v. 33).

The man the Pharisees interrogated kept trying to bring them back to the gospel he knew: *He opened my eyes*. He saw Jesus clearly for who he was—one worthy of worship. That's the goal in witness: to communicate our worship of Jesus, that we are responsive to him. The man Jesus healed knew that worship was reserved for God alone (v. 31). When Jesus found him later and referred to himself as "the Son of Man" (v. 35), all the pieces fell into place. Son of Man was a divine title.[16]

Faith is trust in what we have good reason to believe is true. More than that, faith is trust that worships, and faith that worships will turn into love. The Pharisees bound themselves to self-righteous unbelief when they adopted a no-love-lost policy toward Jesus.

## Unbelief Believes in Self-Righteousness

The religious leaders would simply not face their self-righteousness. This was ultimately why they missed "the light of the knowledge of the glory of God in the face of Jesus Christ." Those words of Paul, a former Pharisee, in 2 Corinthians 4:6 were written in a context in which Paul said Satan blinds the minds of unbelievers in order to keep them from seeing "the light of the gospel of the glory of Christ, who is the image of God" (2 Cor 4:4). C. S. Lewis conveyed an important insight on this in *The Screwtape Letters* when the senior demon, Screwtape, wrote his junior, Wormwood, "It is funny how mortals always picture us as putting things into their minds: in reality our best work is done by keeping things out."[17]

16. See Dan 7.

17. Lewis, *Screwtape Letters*, 25.

Human beings are neither basically good nor basically bad. What we are is *for ourselves* in such a way that sin is always a live option. In her memoir *Surprised by Oxford*, Carolyn Weber describes learning to recognize self-righteousness as sin:

> I could grasp (though of course never understand or condone) remote sins—overt acts of terror or hatred, atrocities flashing across the nightly news in faraway lands or happening to people I did not know. It was the immediacy of sin that was more slippery, the sins right under my nose, under my own skin. I did not understand the pervasiveness of sin—how I simultaneously wove it and got caught in it, and just how far-reaching its effects were. We always assume that its great gnarled roots lie somewhere else; at least I know I did. I always felt certain that someone else was responsible for casting shadows on my vista. The flinging of small pebbles. The dropping of large rocks. The pond ripples out as a result either way, and the waves bring it all back to shore.[18]

Jesus came to bear our unrighteousness *and* self-righteousness on his cross. No one is exempt from sinning, whether our contribution to the whole is the size of a mere pebble in his sandal or the boulder that sealed his tomb. The ripples and waves of sin are caused by us each and all.

It was difficult for the Pharisees to see the sin that sprung from them; difficult due to a high control, high conformity spiritual dynamic they lived out of. That dynamic blinds its occupants to their self-righteousness. When the Pharisees "reviled" the man testifying to them that Jesus' power was God's (v. 28); when they degraded him and kicked him out of the synagogue (v. 34), their unbelief was evidencing itself as belief in self-righteousness. Unbelief does not believe in nothing. It believes in one's own self-righteousness.

There is an implicit *woe* in Jesus' response to the Pharisees in verses 39–41. *Woe* is often heard as equivalent to a curse, but it wasn't. Elsewhere, like in Matthew 23, woes are explicitly

18. Weber, *Surprised by Oxford*, 59–60.

pronounced against the forms Pharisee rejection of Jesus took. When Jesus walked our earth, his toughest words were for those who overemphasized high conformity to an external standard and thereby missed God's heart for people. *Woe* was an empathic cry: *I can't believe how deep your opposition to me goes!*

Jesus didn't tell the Pharisees they were blind to rub their faces in it, but to communicate to them their need for grace and call them to it. Their sin didn't have to have the last word. To see our sin is to see our need for grace. To see our need for grace is to look for a grace giver. There is no better one—no other one—than the one in whom there was no unrighteousness or self-righteousness, ever.

At the core of self-righteousness is thinking we can be our own savior. We go looking in sin—both unrighteous and self-righteous sin—for what we should seek from a Savior. This is why Jesus was hard on the religious leaders: they were so close to grasping God's provision for sin, and yet so far because of their tight grip on control.

The Pharisees have long gone, but unbelief as the Pharisees wore it is still around. Whenever we encounter people, religious or not, who want to be their own savior, trusting their own goodness, self-justifying, we're seeing Pharisee unbelief—unbelief as belief in self-righteousness. And such were some of us. We can remember when we were looking *at* the window, caught up in our religious performance, and not *through* it at the glory of God. In Christ, we now "*see* what we have seen"[19] about ourselves: that without a savior we're bound to unbelief that believes in the wrong things.

Gospel witness is often hardest before those who consider themselves good people. Good people can be as hard as Pharisees to evangelize. I minister in the South, a region not yet post-Christian in culture.

> Religion is a pastime down here. Church is in our blood. If someone drops Christian-sounding verbiage, everyone assumes the best. All the people you see are Christians. Just ask them. They were born into Christian homes. They've never cheated on their wives. They've

19. Dark, *Life's Too Short*, 44–45.

> attended Sunday school since they were young. If you ask someone, "Are you a Christian?" he will immediately tell you where he goes to church. It's all one big ongoing assumption. But biblical Christianity assumes nothing. It conflicts directly with the suburban church. The cross is a vandal down here in our heavily churched neighborhoods, incessantly defacing our facades with embarrassing truths, including, "You are not as good as you think you are" . . . I would argue that the most densely churched spots in this country are in the greatest need of evangelism.[20]

Surprised? Don't be. Look at the Pharisees. Look at the man born blind, now seeing, standing before them, incredulous that they can't *see* it too—the power of God is at work in the person of Jesus! Our goodness gets in the way of our gospel receptors as much as our badness. No one needs to go out and prove how bad he or she could be. But the pursuit of holiness turned the Pharisees in on themselves. It still happens.

God took a man born blind, gave him sight in a most unconventional way, and then used him as a most unlikely witness to good men who could not see—would not see—that Jesus was sent to them too. The gospel goes to good people who feel they have it all together, as well as those for whom the bottom has dropped out of life. The blind man was a prism; a prism is for light to show through. "As long as I am in the world, I am the light of the world" (v. 5).

Jesus still opens blind eyes. He is keen to specialize with those who think they can see.

20. Yawn, *Suburbianity*, 47, 61.

# John 11:1–44, ESV

Now a certain man was ill, Lazarus of Bethany, the village of Mary and her sister Martha. 2 It was Mary who
anointed the Lord with ointment and wiped his feet with
her hair, whose brother Lazarus was ill. 3 So the sisters
sent to him, saying, “Lord, he whom you love is ill.” 4 But
when Jesus heard it he said, “This illness does not lead to
death. It is for the glory of God, so that the Son of God
may be glorified through it.”

5 Now Jesus loved Martha and her sister and Lazarus. 6 So, when he heard that Lazarus[a] was ill, he stayed
two days longer in the place where he was. 7 Then after
this he said to the disciples, “Let us go to Judea again.” 8
The disciples said to him, “Rabbi, the Jews were just now
seeking to stone you, and are you going there again?” 9
Jesus answered, “Are there not twelve hours in the day?
If anyone walks in the day, he does not stumble, because
he sees the light of this world. 10 But if anyone walks in
the night, he stumbles, because the light is not in him.”
11 After saying these things, he said to them, “Our friend
Lazarus has fallen asleep, but I go to awaken him.” 12 The
disciples said to him, “Lord, if he has fallen asleep, he will
recover.” 13 Now Jesus had spoken of his death, but they
thought that he meant taking rest in sleep. 14 Then Jesus
told them plainly, “Lazarus has died, 15 and for your sake
I am glad that I was not there, so that you may believe.
But let us go to him.” 16 So Thomas, called the Twin,[b]
said to his fellow disciples, “Let us also go, that we may
die with him.”

17 Now when Jesus came, he found that Lazarus
had already been in the tomb four days. 18 Bethany was
near Jerusalem, about two miles[c] off, 19 and many of
the Jews had come to Martha and Mary to console them
concerning their brother. 20 So when Martha heard
that Jesus was coming, she went and met him, but Mary
remained seated in the house. 21 Martha said to Jesus,
“Lord, if you had been here, my brother would not have
died. 22 But even now I know that whatever you ask
from God, God will give you.” 23 Jesus said to her, “Your
brother will rise again.” 24 Martha said to him, “I know
that he will rise again in the resurrection on the last day.”

25 Jesus said to her, “I am the resurrection and the life.
[d] Whoever believes in me, though he die, yet shall he
live, 26 and everyone who lives and believes in me shall
never die. Do you believe this?” 27 She said to him, “Yes,
Lord; I believe that you are the Christ, the Son of God,
who is coming into the world.”

28 When she had said this, she went and called her
sister Mary, saying in private, “The Teacher is here and
is calling for you.” 29 And when she heard it, she rose
quickly and went to him. 30 Now Jesus had not yet come
into the village, but was still in the place where Martha
had met him. 31 When the Jews who were with her in
the house, consoling her, saw Mary rise quickly and go
out, they followed her, supposing that she was going to
the tomb to weep there. 32 Now when Mary came to
where Jesus was and saw him, she fell at his feet, saying
to him, “Lord, if you had been here, my brother would
not have died.” 33 When Jesus saw her weeping, and
the Jews who had come with her also weeping, he was
deeply moved[e] in his spirit and greatly troubled. 34
And he said, “Where have you laid him?” They said to
him, “Lord, come and see.” 35 Jesus wept. 36 So the Jews
said, “See how he loved him!” 37 But some of them said,
“Could not he who opened the eyes of the blind man also
have kept this man from dying?”

38 Then Jesus, deeply moved again, came to the
tomb. It was a cave, and a stone lay against it. 39 Jesus
said, “Take away the stone.” Martha, the sister of the dead
man, said to him, “Lord, by this time there will be an
odor, for he has been dead four days.” 40 Jesus said to
her, “Did I not tell you that if you believed you would see
the glory of God?” 41 So they took away the stone. And
Jesus lifted up his eyes and said, “Father, I thank you that
you have heard me. 42 I knew that you always hear me,
but I said this on account of the people standing around,
that they may believe that you sent me.” 43 When he had
said these things, he cried out with a loud voice, “Lazarus, come out.” 44 The man who had died came out,
his hands and feet bound with linen strips, and his face
wrapped with a cloth. Jesus said to them, “Unbind him,
and let him go.”

# 7

# The Problem with Happy Funerals

Though I shall indeed recall that death is being overcome, my grief is that death still stalks this world and one day knifed down my Eric.

—Nicholas Wolterstorff[1]

We tend to think of physical healing in all-or-nothing terms. But there are at least four ways healing happens, not just one.[2] If I cut my finger or get a virus, immediately cells go to work in my body. God made the human body with self-repairing mechanisms. Self-healing, by divine design, is one kind of healing.

The second kind of healing is by divine intervention. No medical explanation will account for the sudden wellness. Doctors are dumbstruck. The lame are now walking, the deaf hearing, the blind seeing. Cancer goes fleeing into remission. God did it.

A third kind of healing is through the instrumentation of medicine. As a result of medical practitioners plying their skills, we are treated, take prescriptions, follow therapies, and heal.

1. Wolterstorff, *Lament for a Son*, 32.

2. Wilson, *Life*, 113–17.

The fourth kind of healing we don't think of as healing but defeat. *He lost his battle with cancer*, we say. But dying in Christ qualifies as healing, in that dying in Christ is the way to the life anew he previewed: "I am the resurrection and the life. Whoever believes in me, though he die, yet shall he live" (v. 25). Ultimate healing. It is never whether God will heal us but when and how.

This is hopeful for Christians. Even though we cannot fully imagine what life after death in the presence of Jesus will be like, we know it is something to look forward to. Alan Lightman is a theoretical physicist who admits to having nothing to look forward to postmortem due to his materialist worldview. But still he longs for something more:

> For a materialist, death is the name we give to a collection of atoms that once had the special arrangement of a functioning neuronal network and now no longer does so. From a scientific point of view, I cannot believe anything other than [this]. But I am not satisfied with that picture . . . I often wonder: Where are they now, my deceased mother and father? I know the materialist explanation, but that does nothing to relieve my longing for them, or the impossible truth that they do not exist.[3]

Death in Christ is existence glorified, our faith finally sight.[4] For this we rejoice in hope, but does hope mean that we cannot grieve deaths? Does it require us to put on our bravest face? Does it require that we tell each other everything is really ok?

Christians can be too quick to leapfrog over grieving; thinking hope somehow requires suppression of pain from searing losses.

> We speak of our funerals as celebrations of life, not the chance to mourn the end of something beautiful or the hole left behind in a web of meaningful relationships. We remind each other that whatever is in the casket it isn't the one we loved. They're in a better place. Nothing to see here . . . Death is the separation of good things not

3. Lightman, *Searching for Stars*, 137.

4. 2 Cor 5:1–9.

> meant to be sundered . . . Death is not ok. By avoiding the subject of death, we act like it's not true.[5]

The losses we suffer when those we love die are *real* losses. That is not "just" a body in the casket. "To suggest in the early going of grief that the dead body is 'just' anything rings as tinny in its attempt to minimalize as it would if we were to say it was 'just' a bad hair day when the girl went bald from her chemotherapy. Or that our hope for heaven on her behalf was based on the belief that Christ raised 'just' a body from dead."[6]

What does hope require of us when the fourth kind of healing is the answer to our prayers? We're told in Scripture not that we do not grieve. We're told we do not grieve as those who have no hope.[7]

## The Undertaking

As a pastor I do a lot of funerals, and funerals are the right place to speak of Christian hope, that the grave is not the end for us. For Christians "there is an Easter out there with our name on it."[8] People will think of their own mortality attending another's funeral. Some families ask me to be sure to present the gospel in eulogy, but they never really have to ask me to. I'm a gospel preacher and know that a funeral audience is particularly reflective, if not receptive.

> Funerals press the noses of the faithful against the windows of their faith. Vision and insight are often coincidental with demise. Death is the moment when the chips are down. The moment of truth when the truth that we die makes relevant the claims of our prophets and apostles. Faith is not required to sing in the choir, for bake sales or building drives; to usher or deacon or elder or

5. McCullough, *Remember Death*, 54–56.
6. Lynch, *Undertaking*, 21.
7. 1 Thess 4:13.
8. Lynch, *Undertaking*, 72.

> priest. Faith is for the time of our dying and the time of the dying of the ones we love.[9]

I've noticed that more than a few of the faithful feel awkward grieving, or in the presence of grieving. For some, it is because they're stoic and stuff their emotions. Maybe they fear losing themselves in overpowering sadness. Some buy in to chirpy ideas of positive confession, that negative words and ideas close off Heaven's blessings or otherwise invite spiritual problems. They consider lament to be negative. And there are always those who drown or dull their sorrows with substances, sadly. It seems that too many have the notion that Christians shouldn't get down or depressed. Like the character Joy in the animated movie *Inside Out*, they try to keep Sadness away from their emotional control panels because they don't understand the purpose she has within us.

In funeral planning with families, sometimes I find that believers want to demonstrate to unbelieving friends and family members that there is a qualitative difference between Christians' and non-Christians' experiences in loss. At times, I sense that believers almost feel a need to deny the sting of death in order to communicate the comfort of gospel-centered hope. Maybe this is a little like trying to ride a bicycle on a punctured front tire.

Additionally, believers often assume unbelievers around us can only gnash their teeth at death and dying. But consider this news story on funeral trends in the UK:

> The British funeral has been transformed. Increasingly, the ceremony pays tribute to the deceased's life instead of mourning their death . . . Death is changing. Now it's a time to be joyful. Instead of looking ahead to the afterlife, British funerals increasingly rejoice in memories of the deceased's triumphs, relationships and their favorite songs. There's a phrase for ceremonies like this—"a celebration of life." The tone is happy rather than mournful, celebratory instead of somber. Wearing black is commonly discouraged. You're more likely to hear Monty Python's "Always Look On The Bright Side

9. Lynch, *Undertaking*, 80.

> of Life"—according to a 2014 survey, the most popular song played at UK funerals—than Verdi's Requiem.[10]

For Christians, our expectation of resurrection due to Jesus' resurrection is a bright side, to be sure. Our enemy (capital "D" Death) has been defanged. To die in Christ is to immediately experience the hope of our salvation in fullness. To be absent from the body is to be present with the Lord.[11] That's always a good word at our funerals.

But death defies image management. It won't be put under our control, try though we might. A character named Mrs. Cobb in Gary Schmidt's children's novel *Lizzie Bright and the Buckminster Boy* tried just that and failed.

Turner Buckminster was a preacher's son commissioned by his dad to make piano-playing visits to the homebound Mrs. Cobb. It was during those visits that Turner learned that cranky Mrs. Cobb had determined to know the precise time of her death and thereby would, before breathing her last, beautifully recite these words: "Safely to the mountains lead me. Safely to my heavenly home. Safely to Your mansions guide me. Never, oh never, to walk alone."

During a visit one Sunday afternoon, Mrs. Cobb neither looked nor felt well. Turner, who'd brought a friend along, Lizzie, played the piano as he was supposed to. Staring into the distance, Ms. Cobb stopped him. Her breathing was labored and she laid her head back against the rest of her chair and recited her precious last words in the children's hearing. She then closed her eyes and was unresponsive to Turner and Lizzie's calls to her. The children argued whether Mrs. Cobb was really dead or not, but as Turner tried to write down her last words for his father's eulogy of her—per her careful instructions on previous visits—he got the order and wording wrong.

A flustered Mrs. Cobb shot open her eyes to tell Turner he just ruined her perfect ending. She would have to come up with

10. Kelly, "Happy Funerals?," paras. 1–4

11. 2 Cor 5:8.

better last words now. She wasn't going to be remembered for anything less than pious prose before being gathered to her people, but now she would have to speak something easier for a boy his age to catch. Then she said, "Oh hell, it's warm here. Get me a ginger ale." As the children went to fetch the drink from the icebox, Mrs. Cobb died in her chair—her last words that ingloriously worded request.[12]

At its best, a Christian funeral speaks God's words, the gospel, over the deceased. Grace gets the last word. It's also a time to express gratitude for our dead in Christ. We can even bask in a winsome personality. One of my father-in-law's best friends was a professor at my university and a folk humorist. He wore a flowing gray beard, which suited his bluegrass banjo-playing and grand storytelling. His memorial service included an open microphone. Person after person, friends from his childhood on, regaled the congregation with hilarious stories of the professor. I've left funerals with my heart hurting, but that one just about busted my gut. The professor was a Christian, and the sermon that followed the stories was gospel-centered and commended his love for Jesus.

There were tears there. Who wouldn't miss such an endearing man? It wasn't that his funeral *had to be happy* because Christian hope supposedly disallows grieving. Funeral trends that veto anything other than celebration of life, suppressing grief and anger at loss, are actually something less than fully Christian. The problem with "happy only" funerals is that Jesus is still a sworn enemy of Death. For now, until Jesus comes, Death rears its ugly head to snatch our loved ones from us.

> If death is not a problem, Jesus won't be much of a solution. The more deeply we feel death's sting, the more consciously we will feel the gospel's healing power. The more carefully we number our days, the more joyfully we'll hear that death's days are numbered too. And the more we allow ourselves to grieve the separations death brings to our lives, the more fully we will long for the world in which "he will wipe away every tear from their

12. Schmidt, *Lizzie Bright*, 149–51.

eyes, and death shall be no more, neither shall there be mourning, nor crying, nor pain anymore" (Rev 21:4).[13]

## The Sting of Death

Death is not merely atomic disbanding, as in a materialist view. Death is not an accident. It's the appointment for every person who sins and falls short of the glory of God. That's all of us. Death is the original tragedy. But this show must go on in a fallen world.

The gospel proclaims the glory of a savior who tasted death himself though he did nothing to merit its sting. When he stared it down in John 11, he fumed at it. It is *suffered loss*. It is not the way this world was supposed to be, and he knew it better than anyone.

When my youngest daughter was seven-years-old we buried her grandmother, my wife's mom. It was painful to lose her piece by piece as her cancer progressed. Brain cancer is particularly cruel. I remember her funeral well. It wasn't until when were seated in the front pew of the church that it finally connected with my seven-year-old why we were there. It hit her full-force—her beloved Grandma, the woman who always had time to read her a story and play dolls and bake cookies—was gone. Tears streamed her face and she said aloud: *I don't want Grandma to be dead!*

Someone has said we want a world without murders but not murder mysteries. We want a world without death too, but not without resurrection. Without death resurrection does not exist. In the Introduction to this book, I wrote that the resurrection of Jesus is *the sign* by which we believe in him and have life in his name. To restate it: I'm not a Christian because I believe Jesus turned water into wine or walked on water. I'm a Christian because I believe Jesus walked out of his tomb.

Lazarus did too, thanks to Jesus' unmatched power over life and death. A personal friend of Jesus, Lazarus got deathly sick. Word about it was sent to Jesus, but he delayed going to his friend at first. His raising Lazarus back to life was the pinnacle point of the seven sign events John recorded for three reasons.

13. McCullough, *Remember Death*, 56.

The first reason is that the raising of Lazarus was the final straw for the religious chieftains who opposed Jesus. Remarkably, it is when he raised Lazarus from death that they said *he's really got to be stopped now!* They sought from then on to kill Jesus. (They even wanted to kill Lazarus![14])

The second reason the raising of Lazarus is the zenith of the seven signs is because John takes care to emphasize Jesus' glory on display in and through his miracles—this one in John 11 is "the gloriest." In verse 4, John records Jesus saying that he would be glorified through Lazarus's illness. Recall earlier in John 9 how Jesus said something similar with reference to the man born blind. And back in John 2 as well, when Jesus turned rinse water into wine, John wrote that Jesus "manifested his glory."[15]

The third reason is because the raising of Lazarus anticipated Jesus' own experience with death to come. The supreme moment of glorification for Jesus would follow at his own death:

> "Father, glorify your name." Then a voice came from heaven: "I have glorified it, and I will glorify it again." The crowd that stood there and heard it said that it had thundered. Others said, "An angel has spoken to him." Jesus answered, "This voice has come for your sake, not mine. Now is the judgment of this world; now will the ruler of this world be cast out. And I, when I am lifted up from the earth, will draw all people to myself." He said this to show by what kind of death he was going to die.[16]

John wanted his readers to connect Jesus' glory to his creative power. He could heal the sick and raise the dead with only a word. He could walk on water. He could turn water into wine. But that Jesus was going to suffer, die, and rise from death himself was also to his glory—the ultimate expression of his divine glory.

That is what makes the gospel unique. "The world's religions have certain traits in common, but until the gospel of Jesus Christ burst upon the Mediterranean world, no one in the history of

14. Keep reading past verse 44 in John 11; read verses 45–57.

15. John 2:11.

16. John 12:28–33.

human imagination had conceived of such a thing as the worship of a crucified man."[17] How could God get glory for himself through *that*?

That Jesus suffered death for us means he was sent by God to do more than just abide with us. He came to substitute himself in our place, to open a definitive way for us to know his love for us. His death is also the means whereby he confirms his unparalleled creative power by way of his own resurrection, which guarantees he will make good on his promise to make all things new.[18] If he couldn't walk out of his tomb as he said he would, then none of his promises would be worth anything beyond historical information. We believe in Jesus not so he'll keep us successful and safe, but because he was sent to reveal the way to God exclusively. That way had to pass through an empty tomb.

Lazarus's sickness took him down. The family wanted Jesus to preach his funeral, but he didn't make it in time, to the sorrow of Lazarus's sisters Martha and Mary. When Jesus got word that Lazarus lay dying, he was a two-day journey from Bethany, a suburb of Jerusalem. Jesus waited two days before making his way there. That was intentional on his part.

Due to the divine power God worked through Elijah and Elisha before Jesus, many Jews in Jesus' culture believed a dead body might be revived up to three days after death. Jesus did it on Day Four. That only added to the marvel.

Why did Jesus tell his disciples that Lazarus wouldn't die (v. 4) and yet he did? Throughout this narrative, Jesus speaks beyond everyone's immediate comprehension. Lazarus did and didn't die (both/and). "Our friend Lazarus has fallen asleep, but I go to awaken him" (v. 11). But then, "Lazarus has died, and for your sake I am glad I was not there, so that you may believe. Let us go to him" (vv. 14–15).

Miracle Max, a comic figure in *The Princess Bride* movie, says, "There is a big difference between mostly dead and all dead." Lazarus was all dead. Jesus wept for him. Four days was past the

17. Rutledge, *Crucifixion*, 1.

18. Rev 21:5.

point of no return in the way the locals thought about it. Martha's plaintive greeting, that if Jesus had come when they called for him he could have prevented it, is nevertheless punctuated with her near-and-far belief in his absolute competency. Her near belief: "Even now I know that whatever you ask from God, God will give it to you" (v. 22). Her far belief: "I know that he will rise again in the resurrection on the last day" (v. 24).

Most Jews affirmed immortality and the possibility of resurrection. Martha believed in the glorification of bodies in heaven and that Jesus could do anything with bodies on Earth. Her belief was well placed. Jesus directed the stone to be taken away. He called the dead man to come back outside, to feel the sunshine on his face again. He did! Lazarus would eat his favorite thing for supper with his sisters that night.

## A Living Conflict with Death

Before Jesus restored their brother to the sisters, he entered into their grieving. The story as John wrote it is highly emotional (see verses 5, 33, 35–36, 38). English translations render Jesus' emotions too tamely. When the narrative repeats that he was "deeply moved" (vv. 33, 38), that word was used in Greek to describe war horses rearing up on their hind legs, snorting before their battle charge.

There is a famous poem by Dylan Thomas that parallels this emotion in its through line: "Rage, rage against the dying of the light."[19] Outside Lazarus's tomb, Jesus wept in empathy but bellowed in anger, because in that Bethany graveyard, he was staring down his archenemy Death. The thing that spoiled his creation now took his friend from him, and though he was not powerless, he was still furious.

It's not surprising to find people getting mad at God when they suffer. God is often blamed. *If God is really there why didn't he stop this tragedy?* Martha essentially asked that very question

19. Thomas, *Poems*, 239.

(v. 21). Why did Jesus delay going to them? His delay was not I'll-get-to-you-when-I-do, but a strategic move in service to revealing his glory.

And yet when he got there he too *felt* anger. Why? It was not at himself for being too late, but at the real enemy—Death. Jesus *hated* death and dying for what it does to the living.

There is a tension to respect in this. For now God allows death and dying. It is for Christians the way to resurrection and life in Jesus' name in fullness. For now God allows sufferings of various kinds. He can even impose suffering if he chooses to, as Job's experience demonstrates. But our sufferings are more often unmerited. Suffering blindsides people God loves, and he *feels* that.

Whatever hurts us is something God categorically hates. In fact, that's what it means for God to be wrathful. God's wrath is his hatred of that which hurts his creation. It includes his living conflict with death.

We shouldn't think of God's wrath as out-of-control ranting and raging. Jesus was incensed at what death did to his friend because death is the effect of sin marring his creation. Sin puts an expiration date on human life, something God invested with his image and likeness. Life was built to last. Death is the signature of sin. "God's wrath is not primarily an emotional state but a forceful censure of sin."[20] And God will finally judge and remove what he hates when he holds court at the end of time.

> So Jesus is furious at evil, death, and suffering and, even though he is God, he is not mad at himself. This means that evil is the enemy of God's good creation, and of God himself. And Jesus' entire mission was to take on evil and end it . . . Suffering in the meantime is often unjust and something God hates.[21]

Jesus entered the grieving scene in Bethany fully. He had a warm embrace and salty tears for the sisters and those grieving around them, but hot anger and salty words for the cause of it. He came to

20. Volf, *Free of Charge*, 166.

21. Keller, *Walking with God*, 137–38.

destroy the power of sin, which fuels the horsepower of death. If he had not done that, or if he had destroyed all evil at once (which we think we want God to do), there would be nothing but destruction for us since we're evil.

If you've ever listened to preaching from John 11, it's likely the preacher said it was good that Jesus specified Lazarus to come out, because Jesus' authority was such that everyone would have exited his or her grave. That has the ring of truth. Lazarus specifically was called out, and only Lazarus came out. In doing this for Lazarus, Jesus previewed what each and all of his friends will experience because of him.

Lazarus came out with the linen burial wrap still confining his body (v. 44). That likely made him kind of shuffle toward the tomb exit. He would need to be unwrapped. In its own way, that is fitting. Lazarus was called back to mortal life. He would die again.

When Jesus was raised, we're told the cloth that wrapped his face was folded up neatly by itself, separate from the linen that wrapped him (John 20:7). He walked out of his tomb unencumbered and unaided. His body could pass through walls between rooms. What's the point of all that? He wasn't going to die again. Lazarus would, but not Jesus. He was and is the glory of God alone personified.

*Do you believe this?* Jesus asked Martha in verse 26. *Did I not tell you if you believed you would see the glory of God?* Jesus asked her again in verse 40. What was the point of those questions? Life is a staging ground for faith. Everyone believes something. To have a relationship with the only true God, one has to look at the person of God in Jesus. We have to go through Jesus to get life that doesn't end at death, to be in on God's future. We get life in his name when we put our life under his.

All of this and more is what it means to believe in one who maintains a living conflict with death. It means that Jesus' power shows up in our living, not just our dying. Wendell Berry called our response to Jesus *practicing resurrection*:

> We live our lives in the practice of what we do not originate and cannot anticipate. When we practice

> resurrection, we continuously enter into what is more than we are. When we practice resurrection, we keep company with Jesus, alive and present, who knows where we are going better than we do, which is always "from glory unto glory."[22]

## An Undying Care for the Living

Lazarus's name has been converted into a term used for a quarantine room—a *lazaretto*. The world in sin is a lazaretto, as it were, but Jesus didn't don a HazMat suit to enter it for redeeming us. The embrace of God shouldn't be the experience of those diseased and dead in our sins of unrighteousness and self-righteousness both, but it is. His care for the living is undying.

In this story, Jesus conveyed his care not only by what he did for the family he loved in restoring Lazarus to them, but in crying with them first. Jesus knew what he would do (because he was divine). He wasn't surprised by his own power. And yet he first empathized with his friends in their pain (because he was human).

"Empathy is the ability to become a naturalized citizen of another person's world."[23] But the thing about naturalization for a lot of us is that it doesn't come natural to us. The elderly preacher in Marilynne Robinson's novel *Gilead*, John Ames, said, "I was much better at weeping with those who weep. I don't mean that as a joke, but it is kind of funny, when I think about it."[24]

"Kind of funny" because it just doesn't come natural to most. But empathy is part of God's nature indelibly. It is equal parts compassion, kindness, and gentleness with those in pain. Jesus' tears were not the tears of one helpless to do anything about it. They were the tears of one who became a naturalized citizen of our world. The God-man did not hide his humanity, but displayed it openly.

22. Quoted in Peterson, *Practice Resurrection*, 8.

23. Aldrich, *Life-Style Evangelism*, 229.

24. Robinson, *Gilead*, 134.

Psalm 16 says of God that at his "right hand are pleasures forevermore" (v. 6). I love that because it means nothing about you or me diminishes God in any way. Nothing about you or me damages him in any way. We cannot harm him. We cannot make him less than he is in his perfections. He never sheds tears of regret over us.

We can lessen our experience of God's goodness when we seek from sin what we should seek from our savior, but pleasures forevermore in his presence is *pleasures forevermore.* God enjoys his life. He is not enduring us. He is the God who "comes to Zion with singing . . . and sorrow and sighing shall flee away" (Isa 35:10). He doesn't have to muster that up.

The prophet Isaiah is also the one who told us that Jesus *bears our griefs* and *carries our sorrows* in addition to covering our sin and shame.[25] For the joy set before him, Jesus endured his cross, scorning its shame.[26] God the Son was carrying sorrows in John 11. But then we think of this scene like the people there did: "Could not he who opened the eyes of the blind man also have kept this man from dying?" (v. 37) In other words: *Why this drama? Why didn't Jesus just prevent this?*

For those in Christ, the sorrows we suffer become invitations to go deeper with Jesus in our faith. I once heard someone say something to the effect that suffering is an invitation to a higher dialogue with God. It causes us to take a personal if not pointed inventory: Do I have a meaning in life that suffering cannot take away?[27]

Not a meaning that suffering can't touch. Suffering touched Lazarus, and his sisters, and all who loved him, even Jesus himself. It's unrealistic to think that suffering cannot touch us. The question is whether we have a meaning in life that suffering can't take away. Martha indicates in verse 27 that she did, and that it was sourced in Jesus himself: "I believe that you are the Christ, the Son of God, who is coming into the world."

25. Isa 53:4.

26. Heb 12:2.

27. Keller, *Making Sense*, 57.

Throughout the centuries of church history, many have had to learn how God makes his gospel surer in us in low times. How he makes us more secure in his grace, and that his unparalleled power and absolute truthfulness is what braces our life. If we have a meaning in life that suffering cannot take away, it means that we've centered our life and times not on personal achievements or connections or resources or better than average children, but on Jesus Christ and the hope of his glory.

Lazarus would die again. We are all Lazarus in that we were dead in our trespasses and sins and have been raised to new life in Christ. G. K. Chesterton put this poetically in a poem he entitled "The Convert":

> The sages have a hundred maps to give
> That trace their crawling cosmos like a tree,
> They rattle reason out through many a sieve
> That stores the sand and lets the gold go free:
> And all these things are less than dust to me
> Because my name is Lazarus and I live.[28]

Lazarus would die again. But he would also enjoy the company of his family and friends again. There is much to endure in life and living for now. But the one who called Lazarus back from death would himself rise, and his life is indestructible.[29] While Jesus' other miracles were designed to get us on base with God through him, the resurrection of Jesus is the one that gets us home.

There is incredible joy held out to us in this. Weeping may endure for the night. Stars go blue. But joy comes in the morning.[30] The bright Morning Star did rise.[31]

> Jesus' death and resurrection have purchased freedom to enjoy what you have even though you know you're going to lose it. Enjoy your vacation even though it will be over in flash. Enjoy parenting your preschoolers even though

28. Quoted by Gerson, "I Was Hospitalized," para. 18.
29. Heb 7:16.
30. Ps 30:5.
31. Rev 22:16.

they'll be grown in the blink of an eye. Enjoy your friendships. Enjoy your marriage. Enjoy your productivity at work. Enjoy whatever health you have left in your body. Of course these things won't last. Yes, it will hurt when they're gone. But they don't have to last to be wonderful. They are delicious, God-given, God-glorifying appetizers for the hearty and satisfying meal that is still to come. They are true and worthy foretastes of the banquet spread for all peoples. And Jesus saves the best wine for last.[32]

32. McCullough, *Remember Death*, 147–48.

# Bibliography

Aldrich, Joseph C. *Life-Style Evangelism: Crossing Traditional Boundaries to Reach the Unbelieving World.* Portland: Multnomah, 1981.

Anderson, Matthew Lee. *The End of Our Exploring: A Book About Questioning and the Confidence of Faith.* Chicago: Moody, 2013.

Arthurs, Jeffrey D. *Preaching as Reminding: Stirring Memory in an Age of Forgetfulness.* Downers Grove: InterVarsity, 2017.

Assayas, Michka. *Bono: In Conversation with Michka Assayas.* New York: Riverhead, 2005.

Bernanos, Georges. *The Diary of a Country Priest.* New York: Carroll & Graf, 2002.

Bowler, Kate. *Everything Happens for a Reason: And Other Lies I've Loved.* New York: Random, 2018.

Brown, Steve. *Three Free Sins: God's Not Mad at You.* New York: Howard, 2012.

Buchanan, Mark. *Things Unseen: Living in Light of Forever.* Sisters, OR: Multnomah, 2002.

———. *Your God is Too Safe: Rediscovering the Wonder of a God You Can't Control.* Sisters, OR: Multnomah, 2001.

Buechner, Frederick. *A Crazy, Holy Grace: The Healing Power of Pain and Memory.* Grand Rapids: Zondervan. 2017.

———. *Telling the Truth: The Gospel as Tragedy, Comedy, and Fairy Tale.* San Francisco: HarperCollins, 1977.

Carson, D. A. *The Gospel According to John.* The Pillar New Testament Commentary. Grand Rapids: Eerdmans, 1991.

Chesterton, G. K. *Orthodoxy.* New York: Image, 1990.

Childs, Betsy. "The Apologetic of Humility." *Just Thinking: The Triannual Communique of Ravi Zacharias International Ministries*, Summer 2004. https://www.rzim.org/read/just-thinking-magazine/the-apologetic-of-humility.

"Chinese Student Sorry after Uproar at US 'Fresh Air' Speech." *BBC News*, May 23, 2017. https://www.bbc.com/news/world-asia-china-40013486.

Cole, Cameron. *Therefore I Have Hope: 12 Truths that Comfort, Sustain, and Redeem in Tragedy.* Wheaton: Crossway, 2018.

Covington, Dennis. *Salvation on Sand Mountain: Snake Handling and Redemption in Southern Appalachia.* New York: Penguin, 1995.

Crouch, Andy. *Playing God: Redeeming the Gift of Power.* Downers Grove: InterVarsity, 2013.

Dark, David. *Life's Too Short to Pretend You're Not Religious.* Downers Grove: InterVarsity, 2016.

DeWitt, Steve. *Eyes Wide Open: Enjoying God in Everything.* Grand Rapids: Credo, 2012.

DeYoung, Kevin. "What We Need Most." https://www.thegospelcoalition.org/blogs/kevin-deyoung/what-we-need-most/.

Dickson, John. *A Spectator's Guide to Jesus.* Oxford: Lion Hudson, 2008.

Douthat, Ross. *Bad Religion: How We Became a Nation of Heretics.* New York: Free, 2012.

Dreher, Rod. *How Dante Can Save Your Life: The Life-Saving Wisdom of History's Greatest Poem.* New York: Regan Arts, 2015.

Elie, Paul. *The Life You Save May Be Your Own: An American Pilgrimage.* New York: Farrar, Straus, & Giroux, 2003.

Epstein, Joseph. *Narcissus Leaves the Pool.* New York: Houghton Mifflin, 1999.

Fenn, Lisa. *Carry On: A Story of Resilience, Redemption, and an Unlikely Family.* New York: HarperCollins, 2016.

Forman, Rowland, et al. *The Leadership Baton: An Intentional Strategy for Developing Leaders in Your Church.* Grand Rapids: Zondervan, 2004.

George, Timothy. "Waiting For and With Jesus." *First Things*, April 3, 2017. https://www.firstthings.com/web-exclusives/2017/04/waiting-for-and-with-jesus.

Gerson, Michael. "I Was Hospitalized for Depression. Faith Helped Me Remember How to Live." *Washington Post*, February 18, 2019. https://www.washingtonpost.com/religion/2019/02/18/i-was-hospitalized-depression-faith-helped-me-remember-how-live/?utm_term=.4ae48631276f.

Grosz, Stephen. *The Examined Life: How We Lose and Find Ourselves.* New York: sNorton, 2013.

Guinness, Os. *The Call: Finding and Fulfilling the Central Purpose of Your Life.* Nashville: W. Publishing, 2003.

Haines, Seth. *Coming Clean: A Story of Faith.* Grand Rapids: Zondervan, 2015.

Hauerwas, Stanley. *Hannah's Child: A Theologian's Memoir.* Grand Rapids: Eerdmans, 2010.

Heim, Knut M. "The Lord Is My Shepherd or Predator?" *Christianity Today,* January/February 2016. https://www.christianitytoday.com/ct/2016/january-february/lord-is-my-shepherd-or-predator.html.

Hood, Ann. *Comfort: A Journey Through Grief.* New York: Norton, 2008.

Horton, Michael. *Christless Christianity: The Alternative Gospel of the American Church.* Grand Rapids: Baker, 2008.

Irving, John. *A Prayer for Owen Meany.* New York: William Morrow, 1989.

Keller, Timothy. *Making Sense of God.* New York: Viking, 2016.

———. *Preaching: Communicating Faith in an Age of Skepticism.* New York: Penguin. 2015.

———. *Walking With God Through Pain and Suffering.* New York: Dutton, 2013.

Kelly, Jon. "Happy Funerals: A Celebration of Life?" *BBC News Magazine*, June 14, 2015. https://www.bbc.com/news/magazine-31940529.

Kierkegaard, Søren. *Fear and Trembling.* London: Viking, 1985.

Koukl, Gregory. *The Story of Reality: How the World Began, How it Ends, and Everything Important that Happens in Between.* Grand Rapids: Zondervan, 2017.

Lamott, Anne. *Hallelujah Anyway.* New York: Riverhead, 2017.

Lewis, C. S. *Mere Christianity.* New York: Touchstone, 1996.

———. *Miracles.* New York: Collier, 1960.

———. *The Screwtape Letters and Screwtape Proposes a Toast.* New York: Macmillan, 1961.

———. *The Voyage of the Dawn Treader.* The Chronicles of Narnia 5. New York: HarperCollins, 1952.

Lightman, Alan. *Searching for Stars on an Island in Maine.* New York: Pantheon, 2018.

Lindvall, Terry. *God Mocks: A History of Religious Satire from the Hebrew Prophets to Stephen Colbert.* New York: New York University Press, 2015.

Lynch, Thomas. *The Undertaking: Life Studies from the Dismal Trade.* New York: Norton, 1997.

Macdonald, Helen. *H is for Hawk.* New York: Grove, 2014.

Manning, Brennan. *The Ragamuffin Gospel: Embracing the Unconditional Love of God.* Sisters, OR: Multnomah, 1990.

McCullough, Matthew. *Remember Death: The Surprising Path to Living Hope.* Wheaton: Crossway, 2018.

McDowell, Sean, and Jonathan Morrow. *Is God Just a Human Invention? And Seventeen Other Questions Raised by the New Atheists.* Grand Rapids: Kregel, 2010.

Millard, Candice. *Destiny of the Republic: A Tale of Madness, Medicine, and the Murder of a President.* New York: Doubleday, 2011.

Moore, Russell D. *Tempted and Tried: Temptation and the Triumph of Christ.* Wheaton: Crossway, 2011.

Noll, Mark A. *Turning Points: Decisive Moments in the History of Christianity.* Grand Rapids: Baker, 1997.

O'Connor, Flannery. *The Violent Bear It Away.* New York: Farrar, Straus, & Giroux, 2007.

Palmer, Earl. *The Intimate Gospel: Studies in John.* Waco: Word, 1982.

Peterson, Eugene. *A Long Obedience in the Same Direction: Discipleship in an Instant Society.* Downers Grove: InterVarsity, 1980.

———. *As Kingfishers Catch Fire: A Conversation on the Ways of God Formed by the Words of God.* Colorado Springs: WaterBrook, 2017.

———. *Christ Plays in Ten Thousand Places: A Conversation in Spiritual Theology*. Grand Rapids: Eerdmans, 2005.

———. *The Jesus Way: A Conversation on the Ways that Jesus is the Way*. Grand Rapids: Eerdmans, 2007.

———. *Practice Resurrection: A Conversation on Growing Up in Christ*. Grand Rapids: Eerdmans, 2010.

Plantinga, Cornelius, Jr. *Beyond Doubt: Faith-Building Devotions on the Questions Christians Ask*. Grand Rapids: Eerdmans, 2002.

———. *Not the Way It's Supposed to Be: A Breviary of Sin*. Grand Rapids: Eerdmans, 1995.

Robinson, Marilynne. *Gilead*. New York: Picador, 2004.

Ronson, Jon. *So You've Been Publically Shamed*. New York: Riverhead, 2015.

Rutledge, Fleming. *The Crucifixion: Understanding the Death of Jesus Christ*. Grand Rapids: Eerdmans, 2015.

Sayers, Mark. *Strange Days: Life in the Spirit in a Time of Upheaval*. Chicago: Moody, 2017.

Schmidt, Gary D. *Lizzie Bright and the Buckminster Boy*. New York: Laurel-Leaf, 2004.

Sheff, David. *Beautiful Boy: A Father's Journey Through His Son's Addiction*. New York: Houghton Mifflin, 2008.

Smith, James K. A. *How Not to Be Secular: Reading Charles Taylor*. Grand Rapids: Eerdmans, 2014.

Spufford, Francis. *Unapologetic: Why, Despite Everything, Christianity Can Still Make Surprising Emotional Sense*. London: Faber & Faber, 2012.

Stanley, Andy. *Irresistible: Proclaiming the New that Jesus Unleashed for the World*. Grand Rapids: Zondervan, 2018.

Steinbeck, John. *The Grapes of Wrath*. New York: Penguin, 1939.

Taunton, Larry Alex. *The Grace Effect: How the Power of One Life Can Reverse the Corruption of Unbelief*. Nashville: Nelson, 2011.

Thomas, Dylan. *The Poems of Dylan Thomas*. New York: New Directions, 2003.

Tolkien, J. R. R. "Eucatastrophe." http://tolkiengateway.net/wiki/Eucatastrophe.

———. *The Return of the King*. The Lord of the Rings 3. New York: Houghton Mifflin, 1955.

Truss, Lynne. *Eats, Shoots, and Leaves: The Zero Tolerance Approach to Punctuation*. New York: Gotham, 2003.

Volf, Mirsolav. *Free of Charge: Giving and Forgiving in a Culture Stripped of Grace*. Grand Rapids: Zondervan, 2005.

Warren, Tish Harrison. "The Wrong Kind of Christian." *Christianity Today*, September 2014. https://www.christianitytoday.com/ct/2014/september/wrong-kind-of-christian-vanderbilt-university.html.

Weber, Carolyn. *Surprised by Oxford: A Memoir*. Nashville: Nelson, 2011.

Wells, David. "The Theologian's Craft." In *Doing Theology in Today's World: Essays in Honor of Kenneth S. Kantzer*, edited by John Woodbridge and Thomas Edward McComiskey, 171–94. Grand Rapids: Zondervan, 1994.

Wilson, Andrew, and Rachel Wilson. *The Life You Never Expected: Thriving While Parenting Special Needs Children.* Nottingham: InterVarsity, 2015.

Wilson, N. D. *Notes From the Tilt-a-Whirl: Wide-Eyed Wonder in God's Spoken World.* Nashville: Nelson, 2009.

Wiman, Christian. *My Bright Abyss: Meditation of a Modern Believer.* New York: Farrar, Straus, & Giroux, 2013.

Wolterstorff, Nicholas. *Lament for a Son.* Grand Rapids: Eerdmans, 1987.

Wood, Ralph C. *Flannery O'Connor and the Christ-Haunted South.* Grand Rapids: Eerdmans, 2004.

Wright, N. T. *After You Believe: Why Christian Character Matters.* New York: HarperOne, 2010.

———. *Following Jesus: Biblical Reflections on Discipleship.* Grand Rapids: Eerdmans, 1994.

Yancey, Phillip. *Church: Why Bother? My Personal Pilgrimage.* Grand Rapids: Zondervan, 1998.

———. *Disappointment with God.* New York: HarperCollins, 1988.

———. *Finding God in Unexpected Places.* Nashville: Moorings, 1995.

———. *What's So Amazing About Grace?* Grand Rapids: Zondervan, 1997.

Yawn, Byron. *Suburbianity.* Eugene, OR: Harvest, 2013.

Zacharias, Ravi. *Jesus Among Other Gods: The Absolute Claims of the Christian Message.* Nashville: Word, 2000.